The Archaeology and History of the Native Georgia Tribes

Native Peoples, Cultures, and Places
of the Southeastern United States

Florida A&M University, Tallahassee
Florida Atlantic University, Boca Raton
Florida Gulf Coast University, Ft. Myers
Florida International University, Miami
Florida State University, Tallahassee
University of Central Florida, Orlando
University of Florida, Gainesville
University of North Florida, Jacksonville
University of South Florida, Tampa
University of West Florida, Pensacola

Native Peoples, Cultures, and Places of the Southeastern United States
Edited by Jerald T. Milanich

The Apalachee Indians and Mission San Luis, by John H. Hann and
    Bonnie G. McEwan (1998)
Florida's Indians from Ancient Times to the Present, by Jerald T. Milanich (1998)
Unconquered People: Florida's Seminole and Miccosukee Indians, by
    Brent R. Weisman (1999)
The Ancient Mounds of Poverty Point: Place of Rings, by Jon L. Gibson (2000)
Before and After Jamestown: Virginia's Powhatans and Their Predecessors,
    by Helen C. Rountree and E. Randolph Turner (2002)
Ancient Miamians: The Tequesta of South Florida, by William E. McGoun (2002)
The Archaeology and History of the Native Georgia Tribes, by Max E. White (2002)

The Archaeology and History of the Native Georgia Tribes

Max E. White

Foreword by Jerald T. Milanich, Series Editor

University Press of Florida

Gainesville · Tallahassee · Tampa · Boca Raton
Pensacola · Orlando · Miami · Jacksonville · Ft. Myers

07 06 05 04 03 02   6 5 4 3 2 1

Library of Congress Cataloging-in-Publication Data
White, Max E.
The archaeology and history of the Native Georgia tribes / Max E. White;
foreword by Jerald T. Milanich.
p. cm. — (Native peoples, cultures, and places of the southeastern
United States)
Includes bibliographical references and index.
ISBN 0-8130-2576-1 (c: alk. paper)
1. Indians of North America—Georgia—Antiquities. 2. Mississippian
culture—Georgia. 3. Indians of North America—Georgia—History.
4. Georgia—Antiquities. I. Title. II. Series.
E78.G3 W54 2002
975.8'01—dc21 2002075505

The University Press of Florida is the scholarly publishing agency
for the State University System of Florida, comprising Florida A&M
University, Florida Atlantic University, Florida Gulf Coast University,
Florida International University, Florida State University, University
of Central Florida, University of Florida, University of North Florida,
University of South Florida, and University of West Florida.

University Press of Florida
15 Northwest 15th Street
Gainesville, FL 32611-2079
http://www.upf.com

Contents

Maps

Foreword

Stuck in a traffic jam on Atlanta's north side during rush hour, I find it difficult to harbor good thoughts about anything. But if I squint my eyes a bit and peer through the automobile exhaust fumes, past the urban sprawl, I can look 2,000 years into the past. There on the banks of the Chattahoochee River is another world, the world of the thousands of Native Americans whose towns once blanketed Georgia.

Few modern residents know of Georgia's magnificent Native American history, stretching back at least twelve millennia into the past and rivaling that of any other state. From the wetlands of Okeefenokee Swamp to the heights of Rabun Gap in the Appalachian Mountains, from the Chattahoochee River at Columbus to the Savannah River at Augusta, Georgia still harbors archaeological sites that attest to its Native American people and their accomplishments. Huge towns like Kolomoki Mounds, a state park near Bainbridge, and Ocmulgee National Monument at Macon are world-class monuments to Georgia's Native American legacy.

In this highly readable book, anthropologist Max E. White brings us the story of Georgia's Native Americans, drawing on a century of archaeological and historical scholarly research. His skillfully crafted, well-illustrated volume takes the reader on a journey from the time of the earliest native peoples to the present. Along the way we learn about the early prehistoric cultures as well as the ancestors of the people known as the Creek Indians, whose settlements once covered much of the state.

Professor White, who has a long association with Native American

viii | Foreword

studies in Georgia, also relates what happened to the ancestors of the area's Native Americans when European countries colonized the state and when settlers from the infant United States of America wrested from them the lands their families had lived on for centuries.

As an archaeologist, I have had the privilege of participating in archaeological projects on the Georgia Sea Islands and on the Etowah River near Rome, Georgia. I have also visited many archaeological sites throughout the state. Those experiences have given me a deep appreciation and admiration for the Native Americans in Georgia's past. Working with Max White on this project consequently has been a gratifying undertaking. I know readers will enjoy the result as much as I have. Indeed, it is just the book to take on a leisurely drive along Georgia's back roads, where you can take time to stop, read, and learn about the state's Native American heritage.

Jerald T. Milanich
Series Editor

Preface

In 1734, one year after General James Oglethorpe had founded the Georgia colony, Tomochichi and several other Indians from his group visited Great Britain. Tomochichi was a chief of one of the local tribes near Savannah, and his visit to London was memorialized in a painting by William Verelst. Sadly, within a few years Tomochichi's people vanished, and European settlers moving into the hinterland were putting added pressure on tribes in areas farther inland.

Who were these native inhabitants of what is now Georgia? What had transpired there in the millennia that preceded European contact and the beginning of recorded history? With no written record, the picture is, and must remain, incomplete, but the last century has witnessed a vast increase in our knowledge of the accomplishments of these first Georgians through the efforts of archaeologists, paleontologists, paleobotanists, and other scientists.

The methods of these disciplines permit glimpses of the past and of some of the ways of life of prehistoric peoples—in the case of this book, the prehistoric inhabitants of what is now Georgia. Here you will learn about their adaptations to changes in climate, their interactions with peoples in other parts of the eastern United States, and their increasing cultural complexity. From nomadic hunters and gatherers to farmers residing in heavily populated settlements, Georgia's native peoples not only survived but thrived over thousands of years. The first Europeans found the area rather heavily populated, but diseases introduced by these visitors spread among the Indian tribes and decimated them. When the English arrived in the eighteenth century, the people they met were quite literally the survivors.

These tribes, principally the Cherokees and various groups collectively identified as Creeks, were caught up in the rivalries of the European colonial powers. The resulting conflicts further decimated Georgia's native tribes and hastened the erosion of their land base. With the elimination of one after another of the European powers, the tribes were left to deal with the new national and state governments of the United States. Despite treaties, the tribes saw mounting efforts to get them to leave Georgia altogether. When the Indian-removal policy became law, and with the active support of President Andrew Jackson, Georgia's remaining Indians were doomed. The thoroughness of the Indian removal of the early 1800s left Georgia with no resident population of indigenous Native Americans. The only Native Americans who live in Georgia today have moved there from other states and represent a number of tribes.

This story of the first Georgians spans thousands of years. It is a story of triumph and tragedy but above all of endurance. The legacy of the first Georgians belongs to us all.

Before looking at the archaeological record, it is necessary to survey briefly Georgia's geography and natural environments, for they played key roles in the lives of the people who once made Georgia their home.

I wish to thank all those who helped make this work possible. I frequently had to refer to secretaries, students, and others for often simple solutions to computer questions. Other individuals contributed to this work through their encouragement and cooperation. I particularly wish to thank Billy Townsend, Patrick Garrow, Mark Williams, Ray Crook, James Page, Deborah Wallsmith, Tommy Beutell, Robert Palmer, Sylvia Flowers, David Price, Gisela Gresham, the staff of the Hargrett Rare Book and Manuscript Library at the University of Georgia Library, the staff of the Piedmont College Library, and my wife, Jeanne White.

1

The Natural Setting

Leaving the pleasant town of Wrightsborough, we continued eight or nine miles through a fertile plain and high forest, to the north branch of Little River, . . . crossing which, we entered an extensive fertile plain, bordering on the river, and shaded by trees of vast growth, which at once spoke its fertility. Continuing some time through these shady groves, the scene opens, and discloses to view the most magnificent forest I had ever seen. We rose gradually a sloping bank of twenty or thirty feet elevation, and immediately entered this sublime forest. The ground is perfectly a level green plain, thinly planted by nature with the most stately forest trees, such as the gigantic black oak . . . whose mighty trunks, seemingly of an equal height, appeared like superb columns. To keep within the bounds of truth and reality, in describing the magnitude and grandeur of these trees, would, I fear, fail of credibility; yet, I think I can assert, that many of the black oaks measured eight, nine, ten, and eleven feet diameter five feet above the ground, as we measured several that were above thirty feet girt, and from hence they ascend perfectly straight, with a gradual taper, forty or fifty feet to the limbs.

—William Bartram, *Travels*, 1955: 56

Georgia's natural environment has undergone many changes over the past 12,000 years as climatic events affected world or regional climates. But not all changes in the environment have been wrought by ice ages or other climatic phenomena. Human beings too have changed the landscape, even before Europeans appeared on the scene to reshape it forever. Native peoples cleared areas for their settlements and agricultural fields; they set fire to the forests to drive out game or to clear undergrowth; they made trails; they made fish traps in the creeks and rivers of the Piedmont and mountains; and they quarried rocks and minerals to make tools and weapons and to trade to people in areas where these materials did not occur.

The most drastic changes, however, occurred after European colonization. The more advanced technology of the European settlers made a noticeable impact on the environment. Whole tracts of virgin forests were cleared, and the erosion that followed led to a devastating silting-up of streams; some game species were driven to extinction; and plants and animals introduced by the Europeans often wreaked havoc on native species. Later, roads, railroads, cities, towns, and villages further altered the natural environment and the landscape, often obliterating the sites of earlier inhabitants. And the process continues.

A brief look at Georgia's natural environment and geography today will help put the archaeological record of the first Georgians in context. In area, Georgia is the largest state east of the Mississippi River. Extending from the Atlantic coast to the Blue Ridge Mountains, it remains diverse in geology, geography, and plant and animal life. (This diversity, even richer in the past, proved ideal for the native peoples, who exploited the land's resources, hunting, fishing, and gathering.) Variations in soil type and underlying bedrock, the presence or absence of water, and other local and regional factors determine which kinds of trees and other plants can grow where. Diverse microenvironments exist in a single region, each containing distinctive plant, animal, and insect life. Thus, uplands, coves, ravines, sinks, springs, north slopes, beaches, swampy lowlands, and river bottoms all host distinctive life forms. Variety is apparent everywhere, and this is true for Georgia's geography as well.

The Cumberland Plateau

The northwest corner of Georgia—Dade County and parts of Walker and Chattooga Counties—is part of the Cumberland Plateau geographic province, which extends through several states. Typical of this area are hills and steep-sided valleys. The flat tops of Lookout Mountain, Sand Mountain, and Pigeon Mountain overlook this part of Georgia. Underlain by limestone and other sedimentary rocks, the region, except for the valleys, has rather thin and poor soil. Its northern portion is drained by tributaries of the Tennessee River, while its southern portion lies in the watershed of the Coosa River.

The Cumberland Plateau province in Georgia was originally covered by a forest where several varieties of oak predominated, along with poplar and American chestnut.

The Ridge and Valley Province

The parallel ridges and valleys of the northwestern corner of Georgia that lie between the Cumberland Plateau and the Appalachians form part of the Great Valley. This geographic feature extends through several states

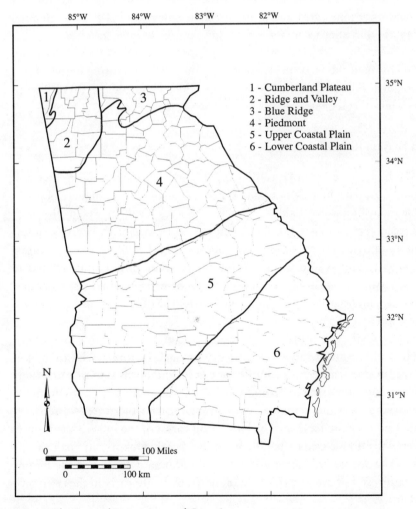

Map 1. Physiographic provinces of Georgia

along the western side of the Appalachian Mountains. A region of sedimentary rocks, it is the location of several types of chert, highly prized by native peoples, for it is easily chipped into tools with a sharp cutting edge. The boundary between the Ridge and Valley province and the Appalachians is obvious, frequently marked by precipitous cliffs on the mountains that tower above the valleys on the eastern side.

The valleys of this province are mostly covered in forest dominated by white oak; along the ridges an oak and pine forest is most common. In some areas oak and hickory varieties more often occur, and in former times the American chestnut grew here. Red cedar dominates the low, flat limestone ridges, forming a unique environment called a cedar glade, a feature that appears in a few places in the Chickamauga Valley.

Most of the Ridge and Valley province is drained by the Coosa River and its main tributary, the Oostanaula. The northern portion of the Chickamauga Valley, however, is drained by Chickamauga Creek, which empties into the Tennessee River near Chattanooga.

The Blue Ridge Province

The Blue Ridge Mountains in Georgia mark the southernmost extension of the Appalachian Mountains. This area includes the highest point in Georgia (Brasstown Bald, 4,768 feet above sea level), as well as the most rugged terrain. That the Appalachians form one of the earth's oldest mountain ranges explains their rounded and heavily eroded features. Ancient igneous and metamorphic rocks occur throughout. Quartzite and steatite (soapstone), both used by prehistoric inhabitants, are found widely, and marble occurs in a few locations. Mica, gold, and copper are also present in some areas.

Originally, this entire region was covered in forest, as it mostly is today. The type of forest, however, varied with such factors as elevation, soil type, and moisture. Cool, moist slopes on the north side of mountains often host northern hardwood species that represent relict communities, for these locations remained cool enough for northern tree varieties to survive after the Ice Age. The hardwood forest of the lower elevations is generally dominated by hemlock, poplar, beech, hickory, and oak varieties. The American chestnut was once a dominant species in the mountain forest, but it was virtually eliminated by blight early in the twentieth century.

Fig. 1.1. The Blue Ridge Mountains (courtesy Georgia Department of Natural Resources)

The Blue Ridge province is included in several watersheds. To the northwest, the area is drained by the Little Tennessee, Hiawassee, and Toccoa Rivers and their tributaries, which flow into the Tennessee River or its major tributaries. Elsewhere, the mountains are the point of origin for the Coosawattee and Etowah Rivers, which form the Coosa River; the Chattahoochee, which empties into the Gulf of Mexico; and the Tugalo, one of the main tributaries of the Savannah River.

The Piedmont Plateau Province

The Piedmont Plateau is one of the larger geographic features of the state. Its high inner edge, known as the Dahlonega Plateau, reaches elevations of up to 1,800 feet above sea level where it meets the Appalachians. Typified by hills and stream valleys with steep sides, the Dahlonega Plateau merges in the south with the Atlanta Plateau, which has lower hills and broader stream valleys. Both of these portions of the Piedmont contain monadnocks, isolated mountains of a very rocky nature. Currahee Mountain in Stephens County, Yonah Mountain in White County, and Stone Moun-

Fig. 1.2. A forest scene in the Georgia Piedmont (photo by David O. Funderburk, Funderburk Studio)

tain near Atlanta are examples. The remainder of the Piedmont is typified by low hills or almost level land. Igneous and metamorphic rocks underlie the entire region. Quartzite is most common, steatite (soapstone) is locally present, and there are isolated outcrops of basalt.

Almost the entire Piedmont was covered in forest dominated by various species of oak and hickory, as well as poplar, pine, and other tree varieties. The American chestnut once grew in the upper Piedmont. River bottoms were often covered in vast canebrakes—thickets of native river cane.

Streams flowing into the Coosa, Chattahoochee, and Tallapoosa Rivers drain the western portion of the Piedmont Plateau. The remainder is drained by the Ocmulgee, Flint, Oconee, and Savannah Rivers and their tributaries.

The Coastal Plain Province

All of Georgia south of the Fall Line, more than half the state, lies in the Coastal Plain province. The Fall Line marks the boundary between the

Coastal Plain and the Piedmont, and it extends roughly from Augusta through Macon to Columbus. It is an obvious geologic feature, as the ancient granitic rocks of the Piedmont end and the younger sedimentary rocks of the Coastal Plain begin. The Fall Line gets its name from the numerous waterfalls formed as streams pour across the hard, granitic rocks of the Piedmont onto the softer sedimentary rocks of the Coastal Plain. Visually, the Fall Line is harder to identify, for the low, rolling hills of the Piedmont extend into the Coastal Plain for a few miles.

At times in the past, the Coastal Plain has been underwater, a phenomenon explained best by Charles Wharton: "The Coastal Plain has been covered by successive inundations of the sea. Numerous fossil localities yield whale bones, shark teeth, and marine shells across the breadth of it. The greatest of these inundations occurred during the last epoch of the age of Dinosaurs, the Cretaceous, which left great quantities of marine sands and clays that we now call the Fall Line Sand Hills. The seashore has withdrawn further during each successive inundation, so that as we drive from Macon to Brunswick we cross younger and younger sea floors and,

Fig. 1.3. A scene in the coastal plain (courtesy Georgia Department of Natural Resources)

sometimes, the remnants of old beaches and dune systems" (Wharton 1978:164).

Although one might not think so, the Coastal Plain is a varied landscape. Along the coast, saltwater marshes and tidal rivers are typical. Barrier islands, often bordered on the mainland side by saltwater marsh, form some of the most picturesque places in Georgia. Inland from the coast, swamps are common. Included is the Okefenokee, the second-largest swamp in the United States. In some areas of the Coastal Plain, gently rolling hills replace the flatlands. Sinks and springs dot the landscape, and each microenvironment hosts unique plant and animal species.

The Coastal Plain is underlain by sedimentary rocks, chiefly sandstone and limestone. Several types of chert occur here.

Apparently, the Coastal Plain was originally covered in a mixed hardwood forest whose main species included beech, several varieties of oak, cypress, pine, and varieties of hickory. Along the coast, tree species include red bay, sweet bay, red cedar, slash pine, and others.

This region of Georgia is drained primarily by streams that flow into the Savannah, Ogeechee, Oconee, Ocmulgee, Flint, and Chattahoochee Rivers.

Georgia's geography and geology and plant, animal, and bird life helped shape the lives of prehistoric and historic peoples, who based their movements on the availability of food, water, and other resources. Archaeological sites reflect the choices they made, and archaeology permits us to know something of the lives of the people who lived in Georgia before General Oglethorpe arrived, and to learn more about those living here in the historic period.

Suggestions for Further Reading

Braun, E. Lucy. 1967. *Deciduous Forests of Eastern North America*. New York: Hafner.

Burleigh, Thomas D. 1958. *Georgia Birds*. Norman: University of Oklahoma Press.

Golley, Frank B. 1962. *Mammals of Georgia*. Athens: University of Georgia Press.

LaForge, Laurence, et al. 1925. *Physical Geography of Georgia*. Geological Survey of Georgia, Bulletin 42. Atlanta: Department of Mines, Mining, and Geology.

2

Georgia's First People

From his place of concealment in the bushes lining the creek, the hunter peered out at a small herd of horses that grazed some distance away. A cool easterly breeze kept the herd from catching his scent, and he carefully positioned his spear on the spear-thrower. Just as he raised his arm to propel the spear at the nearest animal, the whole herd bolted and rapidly moved out of range and out of sight. Perhaps they had caught the scent of a saber-toothed cat, a wolf, or some other four-legged predator. Alert to possible danger to himself, the hunter planned the next move in his quest for food for his family and the others in his group.

This scene could well have taken place in what we know as Georgia some 12,000 years ago, or earlier. Just when the first people, the Paleoindians, reached the Southeast is not known, nor is it known when they first crossed the Bering Strait from Asia. What is certain is that people arrived in North America from Asia sometime during the final glacial period of the Pleistocene. Popular literature refers to the "Ice Age," but scientists know that the Pleistocene (a geologic time period that began approximately two million years ago and ended some 10,000 years ago) has been marked by several glacial episodes of massive proportions. The final such event began about 100,000 years ago and lasted until about 12,000 years ago. It was during this time that modern humans spread to virtually every part of the earth.

In the Northern Hemisphere, a glacial period witnessed the formation of huge continental glaciers that ultimately covered a large portion of northern Asia, northern Europe, and northern North America. As at the present, water evaporated over the oceans and later fell on the landmasses as precipitation. But during glacial epochs, much of this precipitation was frozen and was not returned to the oceans by run-off. This meant a gradual lowering of sea levels worldwide, and at the height of a glacial period, ocean levels were more than three hundred feet lower than at present. Thus, much of today's continental shelf was dry land.

The lower sea levels also meant that Asia and North America were connected by dry land across what is now the Bering Strait. This region was not covered by glaciers, and the remains of animals preserved in Alaska and Siberia indicate that it was a lush grassland where several species of grazing animals roamed. At some time (or, more likely, on several occasions), hunters crossed this land bridge and either made their way down the coast or found an ice-free route to the interior of North America. These were the Paleoindians, ancestors of the tribes the Europeans encountered in Georgia in the sixteenth century.

We do not know how long it took these early peoples to reach the southeastern United States. That they were there in the final stages of the last glacial period is certain, however, for they left evidence in the form of characteristic tools. Fluted spear points are found throughout the Southeast, many either identical to or very similar to those found at sites in the West, where now-extinct animals were killed and butchered. The animal remains were radiocarbon dated to some 12,000 years ago, demonstrating human presence in North America at least this early. Since artifacts found in Georgia and surrounding states are of the same type as those in the West, archaeologists believe they date to approximately the same period.

In a few instances, stone tools have been found along with the remains of extinct animals in the Southeast. In Florida, a stone point was found embedded in the skull of an extinct bison, and a sharpened wooden stake was found with the remains of a now-extinct species of giant tortoise. Mastodon and Pleistocene horse bones that display cut marks from butchering have also been found in Florida, along with tools made from the bones of these Paleoindian prey. These and other finds demonstrate human presence in the Southeast before these animals became extinct, apparently 10,000 years ago and earlier.

What was life like for these earliest Georgians? Imagine a landscape quite different from today's. While the geography was essentially the same, most of the trees, plants, animals, and other forms of life would be unfamiliar. With the lower sea level, the coast would be several miles farther east. Fossil pollen taken from deposits at several locations in Georgia and surrounding states has enabled scientists to reconstruct the forest types of the region during the last glaciation, which is also the period when humans entered the area. The focus of these studies is on the period that begins about 25,000 years ago and included the farthest southward advance of the great North American glacier, about 18,000 years ago. Then a warming trend set in that caused a fairly rapid retreat of the glacier. At its farthest extent, the glacier reached what is now central Indiana and Ohio and stretched across Pennsylvania and New York. As the glacier advanced, zones of vegetation retreated southward before it, creating an environment very different indeed.

Imagine the Blue Ridge Mountains clothed in an evergreen forest composed mainly of spruce and jack-pine. Winters were very long and exceptionally cold. The absence of nut-bearing trees meant fewer animals, and those that lived in the mountains were more typical of environments far to the north today. These included the spruce grouse (a chickenlike bird found today in the evergreen forests of Canada) and the southern bog lemming. In neighboring states, remains of woodland musk ox, moose, and other northern species have been found. The remains of other species that were certainly present have yet to be discovered in the fossil record.

The rolling hills of the Georgia Piedmont were also covered in evergreens, but perhaps as clumps of trees separated by areas of grasses and herbs, as pollen taken from sites in the Piedmont indicate. This parklike environment would have been more attractive to grazing animals, and a fossil site in Wilkes County has yielded the remains of the American mastodon, woolly mammoth, bison, and white-tailed deer, all of which would frequent an area where they could graze or browse. This evergreen forest apparently extended to the vicinity of the Fall Line, where it gave way to a forest of mixed evergreens and northern varieties of oak, beech, birch, and elm that spread southward into the Coastal Plain. Lower portions of the Coastal Plain were home to a forest of southern pine and hardwood varieties that extended into northern Florida.

The animals then found in Georgia south of the evergreen forest formed an assemblage with no modern counterpart. Some, like the woolly mammoth, American mastodon, giant ground sloth, and giant tortoise, became extinct at the end of the Pleistocene. Others survived into modern

Fig. 2.1. Skeleton of a giant ground sloth found in Glynn County and displayed at the University of Georgia (courtesy of the University of Georgia Department of Geology; photo by David Price)

times, such as white-tailed deer, eastern buffalo, and a variety of small game such as rabbits, squirrels, and opossums. Indeed, with the exception of the eastern buffalo, which became extinct in the eighteenth century, all are still found in Georgia. In addition, the fossil record demonstrates the presence of species more common to areas far to the south today, including the jaguar, tapir, and peccary. Thus, the Paleoindians moved into a region teeming with game of many species.

Beyond their surroundings, archaeological discoveries of the past few years enable us to draw some conclusions about the life ways of the earliest Georgians, and to make educated guesses about some aspects of their culture. But the material remains of the Paleoindians are not nearly as common as are remains of later periods, which may reflect a very small population. Also, the older the remains, the longer they have been subject to erosion and other forces that can obliterate or obscure cultural traces. Finally, the archaeology of Georgia is not as well explored as that of some other areas. Georgia is a large state, and archaeological research has been limited. The most complete survey work has occurred in places where reservoirs have been built in the last twenty-five years, and Paleoindian sites were found in several of these locations.

Paleoindian sites are identified by the presence of diagnostic artifacts, particularly spear points with the distinctive fluting. Almost always made from chert, these points vary from one and one-half to five inches in

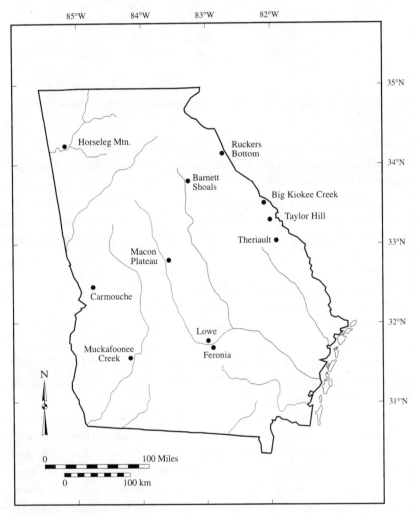

Map 2. Paleoindian sites in Georgia

Fig. 2.2. Paleoindian fluted points from Georgia (from a private collection)

length, with a single flake, or flute, removed from one or both sides. This flute typically extends from the base to about midway down the point. Other artifacts dating to this period include choppers, gravers (a type of cutting or shaving tool), scrapers, microblades, bola stones, and bone or ivory points or foreshafts. The Paleoindian tool kit is remarkably similar throughout the United States, a situation that has led archaeologists to suggest that a way of life based on the exploitation of large game animals prevailed.

The name Clovis has been given to the fluted points and the associated tools. This name is derived from Clovis, New Mexico, a town near an archaeological site where fluted points were found in association with mammoth bones. Also found in the same layer at this site were other stone tools, bone spear points, and camel, horse, and bison bones. Radiocarbon dates for the level from which these artifacts were excavated indicate an age of about 9,200 B.C.

We can make only tentative statements about Paleoindian sites in Georgia because of our limited knowledge. There is increasing evidence, however, that the people who left the characteristic fluted projectile points were not the first humans in the Southeast. Recently, a pre-Clovis level was found at a site in South Carolina, and it has been dated to about 16,000 years ago. Other sites, such as Meadowcroft Rock Shelter in Pennsylvania, yield dates earlier than the Clovis. So far, we know little of these earliest human inhabitants, but we have somewhat more information on the Clovis hunters.

We know that the Paleoindians were hunter-gatherers, and by studying contemporary peoples who follow a similar way of life, we can infer certain things about this early society. On the basis of modern studies of hunting and gathering groups, it is believed that the Paleoindians lived in small groups or bands of probably twenty-five to fifty people who moved as frequently as the availability of resources required. Each band would have established its own territory within which hunting and gathering took place. The Paleoindians located sources of flint or chert, which was highly prized for toolmaking, and trade probably developed with groups whose territory did not offer this material. In Georgia, this stone is found in the Coastal Plain and Ridge and Valley provinces, with isolated occurrences in the Piedmont. Paleoindian artifacts found in these and other parts of Georgia often are made of nonlocal stone. Does this mean trade, or does it reflect extensive travel, possibly following game migrations?

While Paleoindian sites are the least common of all prehistoric sites in Georgia, they do exist, and artifacts typical of this era occur in all parts of the state. Sites of the Paleoindian period appear to be extremely rare in the coastal region, which makes sense when one remembers that the lower ocean level would have put the beach miles to the east of its present location. Thus, Paleoindian coastal sites are now submerged. Paleoindian sites are rare in the Blue Ridge Mountains but are much more in evidence in the Piedmont and Coastal Plain. When we compare site distribution with the occurrence of raw materials, such as chert sources, we find that the Paleoindians located and exploited the material they prized for making their tools and weapons. Their artifacts are widely distributed in areas far removed from the source of the chert from which they are made. Paleoindian sites in north Georgia, for instance, reveal many artifacts made from coastal-plain chert. Local stone, such as quartz, appears to have been little used during this early period.

Recent archaeological surveys conducted mostly as a result of cultural resource–management legislation, have considerably increased our knowledge of the Paleoindian era in Georgia. However, many of the finds have been on the surface, and artifacts belonging to this early period have rarely been found in undisturbed or stratified contexts. Among the excavated sites with a Paleoindian component are Theriault (Burke County),

Taylor Hill (Richmond County), and several sites in the Barnett Shoals vicinity in Oconee County.

Several types of sites associated with the Paleoindians in Georgia have been identified by archaeologists. Sites where stone knives and scrapers are commonly found were almost certainly hunting stations or locations where game was butchered. Such sites are called short-term campsites by archaeologists. Quarry sites occur at sources of chert or other stone and contain tools and debris left from quarrying the stone and manufacturing the tools. Sites identified as long-term or residential campsites are rare in Georgia, but where they have been found and investigated by archaeologists, they have yielded a wide range of tools made of both local and nonlocal material. This variety of tools may indicate either long-term residence or repeated occupation of the same site. Finally, sites where game, especially extinct species, was killed have been found in other states but not yet in Georgia.

No remains of any type of structure from this early period have been found in the Southeast, so we must surmise that Paleoindian dwellings were temporary, probably consisting of a framework of poles covered with animal hide.

Other than the chert used for tool manufacture, we can make only educated guesses about the resources Georgia's Paleoindians used. It has often been assumed by many archaeologists that big game, such as mammoth, mastodon, and giant ground sloth, formed the primary source of food for these people. But this may not have been the case. We do not know how often hunters brought down these animals, but killing one of these large beasts might have been an unusual event. One archaeologist has suggested that it was so unusual that a hunter who killed a mammoth probably bragged about it for the rest of his life. What is virtually certain is that the Paleoindians, like later peoples, relied upon a variety of foods, both plant and animal. While we have little direct evidence (and none in Georgia), we may be sure that they hunted game other than the elephants and other extinct forms. Taking smaller game, such as deer and rabbits, would have been easier and less dangerous. In addition, all hunting and gathering peoples eat some plant foods, and the Paleoindians were no exception. But most of what they and later peoples used is not known, for little information has survived in the archaeological record. Indeed, green plants used for food would leave no archaeological trace.

Many of the known Paleoindian sites in Georgia and surrounding states lie on a hilltop or ridge top overlooking a valley or stream confluence, an ideal vantage point for spotting game and for studying game movements. In areas with no hills, Paleoindian sites lie near shoals or at other locations where game trails probably crossed the river. These sites yield the characteristic fluted points, scrapers, choppers, and other tools associated with butchering and processing and are thus believed to be short-term hunting stations, not long-term residential sites.

As the climate continued to warm and dense forests reappeared across Georgia, cultural changes occurred that are evident in the archaeological record. These changes mark the Late Paleoindian or Transitional Paleoindian Period. The archaeological record reveals a new form of projectile point, which some archaeologists interpret as reflecting a change in hunting strategy. The earlier lance-shaped points, both fluted and unfluted, are thought to have been used to kill large game at close quarters. The spear could have been thrust into the animal, then quickly withdrawn to be thrust again. If a mastodon or other large animal could be stampeded into a swampy or marshy area, it could not maneuver as well and would be much more vulnerable to hunters. But the disappearance of this large game and the return of dense forests would have called for new hunting techniques. The white-tailed deer now became the primary quarry of the Paleoindian hunter.

As Joseph R. Caldwell, a University of Georgia archaeologist, once pointed out, hunting deer in a forest is an entirely different matter from hunting mastodon or other large game in a more open setting. What is called for is a projectile that will remain embedded in the animal and slow its flight through the forest, increase blood loss, and thus improve the hunter's chances of recovering his quarry. The projectile points in the archaeological record of the Late Paleoindian Period reflect this new hunting strategy, for they often have pronounced barbs that would prevent them from being pulled or knocked out of the animal. These are called Dalton points, and from information at the University of Georgia's Laboratory of Archaeology, it is evident that Dalton points are found in all regions of Georgia but appear to be most numerous in the northern part of the state. Since no statewide survey of private collections has been conducted, however, it is too soon to draw any conclusions on the distribution of this and other artifact types.

People making the distinctive Dalton points began to utilize rock shelters in their hunting and gathering, more so than the earlier Paleoindians.

Fig. 2.3. Late Paleoindian
Dalton points from Georgia
(from a private collection;
photo by David Price)

These rock overhangs afforded some protection from the elements and apparently came to be used by hunters on a regular basis. At the Stanfield-Worley Bluff shelter in Alabama, the white-tailed deer was the most common animal represented in the faunal remains in the Dalton level. Other species included gray squirrel, raccoon, rabbit, turkey, and snapping turtle, demonstrating that a wide range of animals were hunted. Also at this site were slabs of pit-marked stone, artifacts typically identified by archaeologists as nutting stones, believed to have been used in cracking hickory nuts, walnuts, acorns, and possibly others. Because rock shelters in other states yield similar remains from the Dalton occupation, it is generally believed that the same subsistence pattern was employed throughout. No rock shelters with a Dalton component have yet been excavated in Georgia.

Based on the excavated remains from rock shelters in several states, combined with a study of open-air site distribution and location, archaeologists conclude that the remains of the Dalton era reflect a changed pattern of hunting and gathering following the dramatic climate changes and animal extinctions at the end of the Ice Age. It is believed that the

If our interpretations of point chronology and site function are correct, it would appear that a full utilization of the Piedmont region did not occur until the latter portion of the Paleoindian period. The earliest sites show a low diversity of tool forms and are restricted to the southern shoals portion of the Wallace Reservoir nearest the Fall Line. The later sites, while apparently still restricted to specific areas of potential site location, demonstrate a wider variety of site types and a greater intensity of occupation. Our data suggest that this increased utilization of the Piedmont by later Paleoindian groups corresponds more to a diversified hunting and gathering mode of subsistence than to a big-game oriented hunting strategy. (O'Steen et al. 1983: 22)

evidence indicates the establishment of the seasonal pattern of local-resource exploitation at this time, a pattern that was to be continued and refined during the Archaic period. While Paleoindian hunters likely exploited migratory game animals to some extent, Dalton hunters apparently concentrated on nonmigratory game, principally white-tailed deer and smaller animals. Shell fragments of walnuts and hickory nuts found in a Dalton context at one rock shelter further indicate use of locally available resources. Radiocarbon dates generally place the Dalton levels in the range of 10,500 to 9,900 B.P. (8500 to 7900 B.C.).

Conclusion

The very earliest Georgians, the Paleoindians, left few traces, and their presence is known from only a few sites in eastern North America. The Topper site in South Carolina is an example of such an early site in the Southeast. Archaeological sites of this earliest period of human presence in the New World have not yet been found in Georgia, but artifacts belonging to the later Clovis hunters occur. Clovis points and associated stone tools have been found in all regions of Georgia, but almost always they are surface finds. Only rarely have these artifacts been discovered in excavated sites, and even then archaeologists believe that re-deposition has occurred in some cases. In very few instances have Paleoindian diagnostic artifacts been uncovered in context in archaeological excavations in Georgia.

Paleoindian artifacts have been found in association with now-extinct Pleistocene animals in Florida, but not yet in Georgia. However, fossil deposits in Georgia are known to contain the remains of animals hunted by the Paleoindians. Two giant ground sloth skeletons have been recovered near Brunswick, and numerous remains of extinct Pleistocene animals have been found on Kettle Creek in Wilkes County and at the Ladd's quarry in Bartow County. Still, no cultural remains have been found at these locations.

The Paleoindian hunters in Georgia and the greater Southeast located outcrops of chert, their preferred stone for tool manufacture, and continued to use these sources for generations. Later peoples also quarried this stone and carried or traded it widely. Archaeologists believe the increase in numbers of sites associated with the Paleoindians in Georgia reflects population growth and more intensive exploitation of regional and local resources. Thought to be occurring at the same time was a cultural adjustment to the changing environmental situation and the extinction of the large game animals. This adjustment took the form of increasing reliance on smaller game and other food sources locally available, as reflected in new technology and in the variety of plant and animal remains in the archaeological record. This increasing dependence on locally available food sources and the establishment of a seasonal pattern of exploitation of resources in different microenvironments set the stage for a period archaeologists call the Archaic.

Suggestions for Further Reading

Anderson, David G., and Kenneth E. Sassaman. 1996. *The Paleoindian and Early Archaic Southeast.* Tuscaloosa: University of Alabama Press.

Begley, Sharon, and Andrew Murr. 1999. "The First Americans." *Newsweek,* April 26, 50–57.

Goodyear, Albert C. 1999. "Results of the 1999 Allendale Paleoindian Expedition." *Legacy* 4, 1–3: 8–13. Columbia: South Carolina Institute of Archaeology and Anthropology, University of South Carolina.

Walthall, John A. 1998. "Rockshelters and Hunter-Gatherer Adaptation to the Pleistocene/Holocene Transition." *American Antiquity* 63, 2: 223–38.

3

Hunters and Gatherers of the Archaic, 8000–1000 B.C.

It was early fall in the hills of the Georgia Piedmont, and the leaves were only beginning to drop from the trees and float to the ground, sometimes hastened by a cool breeze that hinted at the much harsher weather to come. A young woman, along with her mother, her sisters, and some other close relatives, gathered acorns and hickory nuts, collecting them in baskets and bags. They were in the hills overlooking the valley of a fairly sizable river, an ideal place for collecting the nuts that had come to be a mainstay in their diet. While the women gathered nuts near the camp, the men were in the surrounding forest hunting for deer, turkey, and other game. The young woman looked forward to late evening, when everyone would return to camp. If the hunters had been successful there would be fresh meat for all.

She also looked forward to leaving this camp in a few more days to return to a more sheltered location nearer the river, where all the members of her group would spend the cold winter months.

The scene described here has its setting in a time period known as the Archaic, which began some 10,000 years ago (8000 B.C.) and lasted about 7,000 years (to 1000 B.C.). Archaeologists divide it into early, middle, and late stages, set apart by climatic and cultural events. This period witnessed the establishment of some patterns of hunting and gathering that persisted into historic times. Some important technological innovations appeared, including the earliest pottery in North America, and plant cultivation began toward the end of this time period.

The increasing number of Archaic archaeological sites found throughout Georgia not only attests to the success of these peoples in devising hunting and gathering schedules based on the seasonal availability of local resources but also implies population growth.

The Early Archaic (8000–6000 B.C.)

Scientists believe that by the beginning of the Early Archaic, the animal extinctions of the Late Pleistocene were over and modern species dominated the scene. The world climate continued a warming trend begun earlier, and ice masses continued to melt and ocean levels were rising. Sea level was still about a hundred feet lower than at present. The Georgia Piedmont and mountains were covered in the mixed hardwood forest that had replaced the evergreen forest of earlier times. The Coastal Plain had seen a mixed oak-hickory-pine forest take over. Georgia's human inhabitants apparently continued patterns of life begun late in the Paleoindian Period.

Wherever they lived, people went about working out or refining a schedule of exploitation of seasonally available plant foods and devising

Fig. 3.1. Museum exhibit demonstrating use of the atl-atl (courtesy National Park Service)

means of hunting or otherwise procuring game and other resources. Archaeological evidence indicates that this seasonal exploitation of local resources began during the latter part of the Paleoindian Period. The distribution of artifacts belonging to the Early Archaic demonstrates that people lived in all parts of Georgia. Such artifacts are rare along the coast, however. This may be readily explained by noting that the sea level was still considerably lower than it is today. Sites along the coast at that time would now be submerged. In fact, submerged sites from this time have recently been found off the west coast of Florida, so the lack of Early Archaic sites along the present coast of Georgia must not be interpreted as indicating that people of this time were not using marine and coastal food sources.

The Early Archaic Period is marked in the archaeological record by the appearance of projectile points that differ from the Dalton and other earlier types. Apart from projectile points, other tools—stone knives, scrapers, and others—show continuity from earlier forms and are virtually unchanged. It is believed that the projectile-point styles of the Early Archaic developed out of the Dalton types. Although dates vary from one

Fig. 3.2. Early Archaic projectile points from Georgia (from a private collection; photo by David Price)

report to another, archaeologists generally have assigned the following dates to Early Archaic projectile-point types and associated artifacts: 10,000–9500 B.P. (8000–7500 B.C.), Taylor, Big Sandy, and Bolen side-notched types; 9500–8800 B.P. (7500–6800 B.C.), Palmer and Kirk corner-notched types; 8900–7800 B.P. (6900–5800 B.C.), bifurcate-stemmed types, including St. Albans, LeCroy, and others. The sequence of these projectile-point types from earliest to latest has been defined at several sites excavated in surrounding states and at a few sites in Georgia. Some sites yielded radiocarbon dates which, coupled with the stratigraphic evidence, form the basis of the assigned dates. One deeply stratified site excavated in Georgia that reveals many such strata is the Gregg Shoals site on the Savannah River in Elbert County.

This site was located on a high terrace at the confluence of a small stream and the Savannah River. More than nine feet of stratified archaeological remains were found, but massive erosion had destroyed much of the site before excavations began in 1979. Extensive work at this site from 1980 to 1982 yielded not only valuable cultural information regarding the prehistoric inhabitants of this part of Georgia but also geological and ecological records of great interest. Organic sediments from near the base of the deposit yielded a radiocarbon date of approximately 10,000 B.P. (8000 B.C.). Early Archaic levels were found at a depth of eight to nine feet below the surface, stratigraphically well separated from later levels. Artifacts from this early period were made of Coastal Plain chert, Ridge and Valley chert, and locally obtainable quartz. This pattern occurs elsewhere in Georgia, for chert continued to be the preferred material for toolmaking and evidently was widely traded. Among the Early Archaic artifacts recovered at Gregg Shoals was a Kirk corner-notched projectile point.

One of the first Early Archaic sites investigated by archaeologists in Georgia was the Lane Springs site in Decatur County, where a limestone-sink spring gave rise to a creek that emptied into the Flint River. The spring produced such a volume of water that during a flood in 1948, it stripped away a nearby sandy ridge, leaving only the underlying bed of clay. It was on this bare clay that archaeologist A. R. Kelly found "hundreds of worked flints" that had been washed out of the sand ridge. Kelly was in the area checking for archaeological sites that would be flooded upon completion of the Jim Woodruff Dam when he was notified of the artifacts washed out at Lane Springs. Finds from this site included large choppers, end scrapers, an unfluted "Folsomoid" point, and a shoulder-notched beveled point. Kelly noted that most of the artifacts exhibited advanced patination, a chemical change in the surface of chert that implies great age.

One of the earliest projectile-point types of this period in eastern Georgia is the Taylor point, a beveled, side-notched point with basal grinding. Many Paleoindian and Early Archaic points exhibit basal grinding. The function of this practice remains unknown, but it may have helped lessen the chances of the stone point splitting its shaft upon impact. A distinctive artifact called the Edgefield scraper is evidently associated with the Taylor point. Usually made of Coastal Plain chert, it is found, like the Taylor point, primarily on sites in the Coastal Plain of Georgia and adjacent

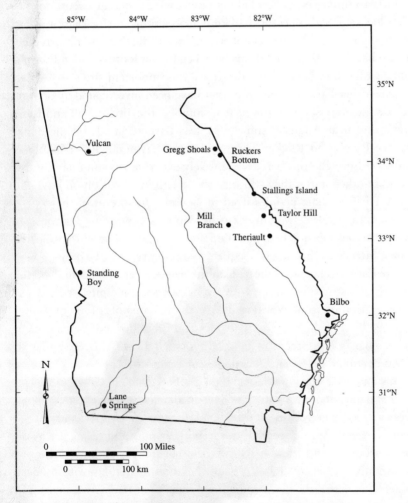

Map 3. Selected Archaic sites in Georgia

portions of South Carolina and Florida. It is rarely found outside the Coastal Plain. Both the Taylor point and the Edgefield scraper were found in the deepest levels of the Theriault site in Burke County.

The Theriault site, an important early site, apparently has now been destroyed by vandals and amateur collectors. On the edge of a swamp on Briar Creek about thirty miles from its confluence with the Savannah River, the site is near chert outcrops, and tool manufacture is indicated by the abundance of chips and flakes present. Excavations there in the 1960s yielded a Clovis point, found just above the sterile clay. The Early Archaic period was represented by several Taylor points, found mostly at a depth of thirty to thirty-six inches. Palmer points were found at twenty-four to thirty inches. Local collectors had known about this site for years and had amassed considerable artifact collections. Some digging had occurred before archaeological investigations were begun, but looting and indiscriminate digging since have all but destroyed this important site.

Some other Early Archaic sites that have been investigated in Georgia include the Standing Boy site near Columbus, the Taylor Hill and Rae's Creek sites near Augusta, some sites near Barnett Shoals on the upper Oconee River, and Rucker's Bottom on the Savannah River in Elbert County. Although none was as extensively excavated as some sites of this period in other states, they still furnish us with information on how and where Early Archaic peoples lived in Georgia. In several of these sites, Paleoindian material was overlain by deposits containing Dalton, Big Sandy, Kirk corner-notched, and bifurcate-stemmed varieties of projectile points, further confirming the sequence of point types in Georgia.

One Early Archaic site, the Vulcan site near Cartersville, contained the remains of a structure. Along with a rock hearth, some pits, and a dense concentration of stone-working debris, the remains of a type of shelter could be discerned. A few large stones and mounded soil defined what archaeologists interpreted to be a temporary tentlike shelter similar to structures found on Early Archaic sites in Tennessee.

To summarize our knowledge of the Early Archaic in Georgia, we can say that bands of hunter-gatherers lived in all regions of the state, moving frequently as game became depleted and plant foods in the vicinity of the campsite were used up. Some foods, especially nuts and fruits, are available seasonally, and these early peoples scheduled their movements to correspond to their availability, if we may use an analogy with modern hunters and gatherers. Plant and animal remains at Early Archaic sites in other states certainly indicate such a pattern. At the Russell Cave site in

Fig. 3.3. A pitted "nutting stone" (courtesy Laboratory of Archaeology, Department of Anthropology, University of Georgia; photo by David Price)

northeastern Alabama, the Early Archaic deposit contained the remains of deer, gray squirrel, peccary, box turtle, and shellfish, and a bone fishhook indicates that fish was also a part of the diet. The author of the site report says that all indications are that Russell Cave was occupied on a seasonal basis by a small band of hunter-gatherers.

Very little of the material culture of Early Archaic peoples remains in the archaeological record. Basketry, leather items, and wooden implements have all disintegrated, except in unusual environments such as peat bogs or dry caves. Even seeds and nut fragments are rare in sites of this early period. Most of what remains for the archaeologist to study are the stone tools left by these early inhabitants of Georgia.

While comprehensive data on the Early Archaic of Georgia do not exist, we can glean some knowledge from various archaeological surveys of the past several years. In addition, site files at the University of Georgia provide further details on the distribution of recorded sites. All these sources show that Early Archaic sites are found throughout the state, but they may be more numerous in the northern part. The inadequate state of our knowledge is reflected in the suggestions of some archaeologists that the Early Archaic is poorly represented in the Coastal Plain. However, a survey of the Feronia locality in Coffee County revealed sixteen Paleoindian or Early Archaic sites in a rather small area. At Chatterton Springs, also in Coffee County, eleven Early Archaic sites were found. Surveys in Pierce and Ware Counties recorded sixty-two Early Archaic sites, and thirty-nine such sites have been identified at the Fort Benning Military

Reservation near Columbus. So it is too soon to draw any firm conclusions about the distribution of Early Archaic sites in Georgia, except to note that they occur statewide.

Middle Archaic (6000–3000 B.C.)

The Middle Archaic Period coincides with the Altithermal, a climatic event during which the Southeast was much drier than it is today. Pollen studies conducted on sediments from natural lakes, bogs, and swamps in the region demonstrate that the forest cover was changing. In the Coastal Plain, pine and swamp vegetation was gradually replacing the predominantly oak and herb vegetation. Studies of these sediments further indicate that the period dating to about 6000 B.C. saw colder winters and warmer summers and less precipitation than at present. By about 3000 B.C., or the end of Middle Archaic times, the climate had evolved to about what it is today.

The Middle Archaic is marked in the archaeological record by the appearance of distinctive projectile point types (Stanly, Morrow Mountain, and Guilford), along with axes and other stone implements that have been ground smooth. The Stanly projectile point type has been dated to about 5800 B.C. at a site in east Tennessee, Morrow Mountain types to about 5000 B.C., and Guilford points from about 4000 B.C., since they follow Morrow Mountain types in excavated sequences in North Carolina and elsewhere. Antler atl-atl hooks are associated with the Middle Archaic, for they first appear in the archaeological record associated with Morrow Mountain points at the Eva site in Tennessee and at the Stanfield-Worley Bluff shelter in Alabama.

One readily observable change in Middle Archaic remains is the increasing reliance on quartz for toolmaking throughout the Piedmont and mountains of Georgia, where the stone is locally abundant. Morrow Mountain projectile point types are almost always made of this material. So common are Morrow Mountain sites throughout the Piedmont that Joseph R. Caldwell introduced his concept of the "Old Quartz Culture," believing that it represented forest nomadism, an adaptation to living in the forest of the Piedmont and using local resources for most needs.

Another artifact that appears in the Middle Archaic is the bannerstone or atl-atl weight, typically made of soapstone but occasionally of other stone. They come in various shapes and sizes, and most are well polished. Their use on the atl-atl has been documented by discoveries in Archaic

Fig. 3.4. Morrow Mountain projectile points of the Middle Archaic (courtesy Laboratory of Archaeology, Department of Anthropology, University of Georgia; photo by David Price)

Period graves in Kentucky, where they were found still in place on the remains of the weapon. However, not all bannerstones are believed to have had a utilitarian function. Some are elaborately made, and some are so heavy that their use with a simple atl-atl seems unlikely. (Some unfinished bannerstones from the Savannah River Valley weigh several pounds each.) Some archaeologists have suggested that such objects were prestige items not intended for use.

Other types of artifacts that appear in the archaeological record in Middle Archaic times include engraved bone pins, grooved axes, and perforated soapstone slabs. While grooved and polished stone axes largely replaced the celts (smooth ungrooved stone axes) of earlier times, another type of implement is also found in Middle Archaic contexts. Chipped-stone axes are found in association with the Guilford projectile points, demonstrating that not all axes were ground and smoothed or polished. The perforated soapstone slabs, because they were at first believed to have served as weights on fishing nets, were called net sinkers. However, at

Fig. 3.5. Chipped-stone ax and Guilford projectile points, Middle Archaic (courtesy Laboratory of Archaeology, Department of Anthropology, University of Georgia; photo by David Price)

Fig. 3.6. Perforated soapstone slabs (from a private collection; photo by David Price)

several sites in Georgia and other states, it has been demonstrated that they were used in what archaeologists refer to as "fireless cooking," a process in which a skin bag or a watertight basket was first filled with the ingredients for a soup. The slabs were heated in a nearby fire and, when hot, were removed from the fire and dipped into the container of soup, causing it to boil briefly. The process was repeated until the food was cooked. Soapstone, a good heat conductor, was ideal for this purpose. Obviously, this rather cumbersome method of cooking preceded the invention of clay cooking vessels in the Late Archaic.

During the Middle Archaic, shell deposits began to appear along the larger rivers, particularly near shoals. Archaeologists in the past had believed that freshwater mussels became more accessible to groups of hunter-gatherers because the dry conditions of the Altithermal meant lower water levels in the rivers throughout the region, which made it much easier for people to wade out in the shallows near shoals and collect the mussels. As they discarded the shells after their meals, large deposits formed over the years. Now, archaeologists are not so certain that this was the case and debate the importance of mussels to people of this time. Along the Tennessee River in northern Alabama, some shell deposits up to eight feet deep covered several acres, indicating that mussels were a major resource in this area. In Georgia, no such massive shell accumulations are known, although there are shell middens and deposits in some locations along the Savannah, Ocmulgee, Chattahoochee, and other rivers. It is believed that freshwater mussels formed a seasonal food of some importance for the people who lived where mussels occurred in abundance, and this might have led to longer-term residence at one location. For groups far from the larger rivers, life apparently went on much as before. The development of longer-term residence in some areas might have led to other changes that took place in the Late Archaic.

Late Archaic (3000–1000 B.C.)

Archaeologists understand the Late Archaic Period more fully than previous time periods, for sites belonging to this period are among the best studied sites in Georgia. The widespread distribution of artifacts associated with the Late Archaic suggests that the population of Georgia was quite large in this period. Distinctive artifacts are found statewide and in all environments, a testimony to the success of Middle Archaic populations in exploiting the natural foods to be found and in working out patterns of movement attuned to collecting resources in various parts of each band's territory. Intensive use of shellfish along the major rivers continued into the Late Archaic but declined abruptly toward the end of the period. Some archaeologists attribute this decline to the rising water level of the rivers throughout the area, a response to increasingly wetter conditions. By the end of this period, both the climate of the Southeast and its forest types were essentially the same as those we see today.

Late Archaic peoples were evidently involved in quarrying and working soapstone into useful implements to a greater extent than earlier peoples. In addition to the highly polished atl-atl weights, they began to fashion cooking vessels from this material. Soapstone outcrops occur in the Piedmont and mountains of Georgia, and in some places unfinished bowls and other evidence of prehistoric activity can still be seen. One of the best-known quarries is Soapstone Ridge, near Atlanta, where archaeologists from Georgia State University gathered much information about prehistoric quarrying techniques. We know that soapstone bowls were chipped out of a boulder or exposed bedrock with a quartz pick. Once the bowl was roughed out, it was detached from the rock and then hollowed out. Finally, it might be smoothed on one or both surfaces. Such cooking vessels were traded widely, for fragments have been found in the Coastal Plain, far removed from the source of the soapstone. While soapstone vessels were being used in parts of northern Georgia as early as 2000 B.C., they apparently were not being used in the Savannah River valley prior to the introduction of pottery. Pottery was being made on the Georgia coast

Fig. 3.7. Soapstone bowl fragments (courtesy Laboratory of Archaeology, Department of Anthropology, University of Georgia; photo by David Price)

as early as 2500 B.C., and one archaeologist raises some interesting questions concerning the spread of pottery and its relation to soapstone technology (see Sassaman 1996).

Some of our most extensive knowledge of life in Georgia in Late Archaic times comes from the Stalling's Island site. This site in the Savannah River near Augusta contained a shell deposit that measured 512 by 300 feet in 1929, when extensive excavations were undertaken. These and later excavations revealed a cultural deposit from fifty-four to seventy-six inches deep, overlying a natural clay base.

At first it seemed difficult to attribute this covering of the mound to the accidental work of man, but the continued study of this deposit eliminated any doubts. It was impossible to discover a square foot of this covering layer that did not contain numerous testimonials in the form of charcoal, food bones, potsherds, discoloration, storage pits, shells, etc. This interesting cultural deposit is the result of a long period of occupation by one tribe, who for convenience will be called Stalling's Island people. After the main period of occupation, other tribes visited the island and lived on the mound. These later people did not stay sufficiently long to build up any cultural deposit of their own, possibly only using the mound as a convenient camp site while on fishing expeditions. However, they did leave potsherds, a few artifacts, and several burials as sufficient proof of their presence. No data were obtained which would even justify a guess as to how many years this refuse layer was in the making. The deposits of shell in themselves are sufficient evidence of long periods of occupation. The sides of the mound are covered with layers of shells, as well as a considerable portion of the mound itself northwest of Trench 2. Although innumerable shells are scattered throughout the cultural deposit covering the southeastern portion of the mound, there is no well defined shell layer until nearing the sides, when gradually definite layers take shape, increasing in thickness as they spread over the sides. It is only natural that the occupants of the mound threw their refuse over the sides, thus surrounding their house site with vast masses of these food shells. (Claflin 1931:7–8; reprinted courtesy of the Peabody Museum, Harvard University)

> The people inhabiting Stalling's Island made extensive use of bone for the manufacture of various articles, as evidenced by the large number of bone objects found throughout the excavations. Nearly five hundred articles of bone were found, many being still in the process of manufacture, ranging from the first rough cutting on an antler to the finished product. No segregation of types occurred either in certain sections of the mound or with the burials. The most common materials used were the leg bones and antlers of the deer. (Claflin 1931:21–22; reprinted courtesy of the Peabody Museum, Harvard University)

Fireplaces and pits encountered in the course of excavation hinted at the location of structures, but no postholes or other remains of dwellings were found. However, animal bones indicated a rather diverse diet. Deer bones were found in large quantities, but also scattered throughout the midden were bones of raccoon, turkey, rabbit, squirrel, fox, and beaver. Quantities of sturgeon, garfish, and turtle bones were also present. The quantity of shells demonstrated, however, that freshwater mollusks were a dietary staple for these people.

Bone tools formed one of the largest categories of artifacts recovered at Stalling's Island, identified mostly as awls or needles. Other tools included deer-antler implements used to work stone, particularly flakers, and some hafts for stone knives. Two bone fishhooks were recovered in the excavations.

The few objects found that were made of shell were encountered in burial contexts—a conch-shell drinking cup, beads, three gorgets, and three earplugs. The beads, from a string more than ten feet long, were found scattered among the remains of two burials.

Bannerstones (atl-atl weights), which formed the largest category of ground-stone artifacts, were found in all stages of manufacture. The winged, or butterfly, form was the most common. Eighteen grooved axes or fragments of axes were found in the excavations. Most were fully grooved, but some bore the three-quarter groove.

The excavations yielded two types of soapstone objects, identified at the time as net sinkers. One type was a rough soapstone lump encircled by a groove; the other was a flat perforated slab. While the former may indeed have been used as net sinkers, we now know that the perforated slabs were used in fireless cooking. More than 2,500 of these cooking stones were recovered in the 1929 excavations at Stalling's Island.

One of the most important discoveries at Stalling's Island was pottery. Lower levels of the site contained none, but pottery appears in levels dated to about 2500 B.C., believed to represent some of the earliest pottery in North America. We now know that its distribution extends along the Georgia and South Carolina coasts northward to the Charleston area and southward along the coast of Florida to the St. Johns River area and farther south. Pottery making extended up the Savannah River to Stalling's Island and is only rarely found farther north. This earliest Stalling's Island pottery was plain, undecorated, and fiber tempered, that is, with vegetal fiber mixed with the clay as a binder. Here and elsewhere, the fiber is believed to be Spanish moss or palmetto fiber, among other substances. In time, the pottery at Stalling's Island began to be decorated with punctations—circles made by pressing a hollow reed into the clay—and incised designs. Still later, linear punctations—stab-and-drag decoration—was used. Some vessels were tempered with shell, sand, or clay. Stylistic or tempering variations have led archaeologists to distinguish several types

Fig. 3.8. Fiber-tempered pottery exhibiting punctate or "stab-and-drag" decoration (courtesy Piedmont College; photo by David Price)

of this earliest pottery: Stalling's Island, along the Savannah River; Thom's Creek, along the South Carolina coast and into the Coastal Plain; St. Simon's, along the Georgia coast; and Orange, in northeastern Florida.

The invention of clay cooking vessels was an innovation of major significance. Clay was both more abundant than soapstone and easier to work with, and clay vessels were lighter than stone vessels. Pottery was durable, and containers could be replaced more easily than could soapstone utensils. As knowledge of pottery making spread, soon people all along the Georgia coast and adjacent portions of South Carolina and Florida were making clay vessels.

One artifact encountered in the excavations at Stalling's Island has since come to be a diagnostic artifact of the Late Archaic, the Savannah River point. These often large projectile points have a square stem. Archaeologists have suggested that the largest may have been hafted knives rather than projectile points, since their size and weight would seem too great for use on a projectile. Especially in the Piedmont and mountains, these large points are made of quartz and are to be found on most sites. That this Late Archaic point is found so widely throughout the region leads archaeologists to believe the area had a substantial population at this time. Smaller points with rounded stems were also found in the same levels at the Stalling's Island site.

Another site that has told us much about life in Georgia in Late Archaic

Fig. 3.9. Savannah River projectile points of the Late Archaic (from a private collection; photo by David Price)

times is the Bilbo site near Savannah. Excavated by Joseph R. Caldwell in the 1930s, the site was in a tidal swamp that drainage operations had turned into a pasture. It consisted of a low mound composed of midden accumulation, more than six feet deep in the center of the deposit. Caldwell found the earliest layer, ten to twenty inches thick, to be composed of oyster shells, presumably discarded after meals. Also in this level were some artifacts, including a bone awl, a perforated soapstone slab, and a perforated conch shell.

Immediately above this earliest layer was a layer containing some fiber-tempered pottery, as well as numerous artifacts of chipped flint and bone. The Savannah River projectile point type was prominent among the artifacts from this level. Also, several clay-lined pits were found. Separated from this level by a layer of river gravel a foot or more thick were hard-packed layers of mussel and oyster shell, sand, and ash. These layers also contained animal bone, flint and bone artifacts, and numerous potsherds of both plain and decorated fiber-tempered pottery. The final deposit at the Bilbo site, the plow zone, contained nails and other debris from the historic period, as well as some artifacts from the late prehistoric period.

The Bilbo site is important because it enabled archaeologists to establish the sequence of fiber-tempered pottery types in the area around the mouth of the Savannah River. The animal and plant remains give us some idea of how people lived in this part of Georgia during Late Archaic times. The site is situated in an area where people could exploit the freshwater swamp and the saltwater marsh for food. Their success is evident by the presence of deer, turtle, and sturgeon bones and mollusk shells. Hickory nut fragments indicate gathering activities beyond the swamp/marsh microenvironment.

Because Late Archaic peoples were hunter-gatherers, we have assumed that they lived in temporary shelters or some type of small, insubstantial dwelling. But recent finds indicate that we may be wrong, at least in some cases. While these people probably did construct temporary shelters, especially at short-term camps, they also built much more sophisticated dwellings. At a Late Archaic site in the middle Savannah River valley, archaeologists found the remains of five structures, one of which might have been mud covered. One of the most interesting finds was a pit-house excavated at the Mill Branch site in Warren County. The floor of this structure was more than a foot below the surface and measured some twelve by fifteen feet. Since there was a large accumulation of ash and charcoal around the hearth, the archaeologists concluded that it was occupied either for a long period of time or repeatedly, perhaps on a seasonal basis. More than 7,000 artifacts were recovered from this structure, including Savannah River points, bannerstone fragments, and perforated soapstone slabs. Radiocarbon dates indicate that the pit-house dates to about 1850 B.C.

In studying the prehistory of an area, mysteries always remain, questions for which we have no answers. One such enigma in Georgia concerns petroglyphic rocks. Scattered throughout the Piedmont and mountains are boulders or groups of boulders that bear markings, drawings, and other evidence of human workmanship. Archaeologists have yet to find anything associated with these boulders that would help to assign them to a particular time period. Still, because Late Archaic peoples were quarrying and working with soapstone and most of the petroglyphs are on soapstone boulders, some archaeologists believe that these artifacts might date to this time period. As one archaeologist has observed, it is easier to say what the petroglyphs are not than to say what they are. They are not a type of writing. Neither are they treasure maps.

The historic Indians of the region knew no more about these petroglyphic boulders than we do, although some devised stories to account for them. Mooney, in his monumental work on the Cherokees, has this to say regarding the petroglyphs at Track Rock Gap: "The Cherokee have various theories to account for the origin of the carvings, the more sensible Indians saying that they were made by hunters for their own amusement while resting in the gap. Another tradition is that they were made while the surface of the newly created earth was still soft by a great army of birds and animals fleeing through the gap to escape some pursuing danger from the west—some say a great 'drive hunt' of the Indians" (1900: 418–19).

Petroglyphs in Georgia generally consist of lines, dots, circles, and tracks, including carvings that resemble turkey, bear, or human footprints. One unusual boulder recently discovered in the Chattahoochee National Forest in Habersham County is covered in lines and dots.

On the Georgia coast, the Late Archaic saw intensive use of coastal resources. Shell middens appear about 2200 B.C., along with features referred to as shell rings. Shell rings are circular deposits of shells and have been interpreted as ceremonial in nature, but some archaeologists maintain that the rings formed when shells were discarded after meals and accumulated near or around living areas. Such features are generally 30–

Fig. 3.10. Old photograph of a petroglyphic boulder at Trackrock Gap, Union County (courtesy Robert Palmer)

50 feet wide at the base, 2–10 feet high, and 130–200 feet in diameter. Usually, the interiors of these rings contain no artifacts; archaeologists have found only a few postholes, indicating a structure. The origin and function of shell rings remain a mystery.

Finally, an important development in the Late Archaic in eastern North America was plant domestication. Even in Middle Archaic times, people in some areas cultivated and grew gourds, but in the Late Archaic these efforts extended to other plants, including the sunflower. Although the plant is native to the upper Midwest, sunflower remains have been found in Late Archaic contexts in east Tennessee. Squash was also being grown in the Tennessee-Kentucky area during the Late Archaic. Other plant remains in the archaeological record of this time include maygrass, knotweed, amaranth, and chenopodium, all known to have been cultivated if not domesticated during succeeding time periods. As yet, there is little direct evidence for the cultivation of plants in Georgia during the Late Archaic, but archaeologists believe that people in the area were also experimenting with gardening. This would have provided an additional source of food, and living in long-term campsites made the growing of plant foods possible. This same situation was true for the next time period, the Woodland, for domesticated or cultivated plants continued to provide an addition to the diet but remained relatively unimportant, even with the addition of corn (maize).

Conclusion

We have now traced the early Georgians through a lengthy and important prehistoric time period known as the Archaic. In its beginning at about 8000 B.C., the climate was changing as the glacial period waned and a more modern situation developed. Still, the environment would hardly be recognizable today, as there were different species of trees, plants, and animals, only a few of which would be familiar to us. Bands of hunters and gatherers displayed that unique human ability to adapt in order to survive, and survive they did. They were so successful in locating sources of food and in working out a schedule designed for efficient exploitation of seasonally available foods that some of their practices lasted into the historic period, having been followed by succeeding peoples for thousands of years. The human population began to increase so that by the end of the Archaic, people were living in every part of Georgia. Important technological advances were made during the Archaic, not the least of which was the making of pottery. Also during the Archaic we find the first evidence of agriculture—or, more accurately, horticulture, for it was of limited scope and apparently contributed little to their overall diet. The basic hunting-fishing-gathering-gardening way of life persisted into the next time period, but other changes were occurring.

Suggestions for Further Reading

Bense, Judith A. 1994. *Archaeology of the Southeastern United States*. San Diego: Academic Press.

Clausen, C. J., A. D. Cohen, Cesare Emiliani, J. A. Holman, and J. J. Stipp. 1979. "Little Salt Spring, Florida: A Unique Underwater Site." *Science*, February 16, 609–14.

DePratter, Chester B. 1975. "The Archaic in Georgia." *Early Georgia* 3, 1: 1–16.

Sassaman, Kenneth E., and David G. Anderson, eds. 1996. *Archaeology of the Mid-Holocene Southeast*. Gainesville: University Press of Florida.

4

The Woodland Period, 1000 B.C.–A.D. 1000

The children and a few grownups waited expectantly on the riverbank as the dugout approached the shore. They had heard that these strangers from far to the north were on their way downriver and would soon visit their village again. It was not the first time they had visited, but the people were always full of wonder and curiosity concerning the visitors. The central figure in the dugout, obviously an important person, was elaborately painted, wore his hair in a bun, and was dressed in a short black kilt-like garment. These people always stopped here on their way downriver and again as they made their way back, the dugout laden with shells and other exotic goods obtained from the tribes along the coast.

One reason for their visit was, undoubtedly, because several seasons earlier, one of them had died here, and the other members of the group had erected a mound of earth and stones over his tomb. Their rites were strange and wonderful to behold, making the local people wonder what the settlements were like where these strangers originated and what elaborate ceremonies they must hold there.

Such a scene could well have been played out along the Chattahoochee River in what is now west Georgia during a period called the Woodland.

The visitors in this vignette are members of the Hopewell culture, centered in the Ohio Valley. Archaeologists debate whether such direct contact occurred, but we do know that Hopewellian influence reached as far south as the Gulf Coast, and Hopewell burial mounds and associated artifacts have been found in Georgia. But before discussing this, we must look at the course of events during the Early Woodland.

For the Archaic Period, changes in projectile point forms are the primary indicators for time divisions into Early, Middle, and Late Archaic. Other technological changes might help to determine temporal affiliation of a site, but in the Woodland Period, beginning about 1000 B.C., pottery becomes the archaeologists' primary tool for establishing sub-periods.

Pottery came into wide use throughout the Southeast in the Early Woodland Period, and distinctive vessel forms, decoration, and other attributes are good indicators of time sequences. When archaeologists can obtain a radiocarbon date on material associated with a distinctive style of pottery, they can assign a date for its manufacture. When an excavated

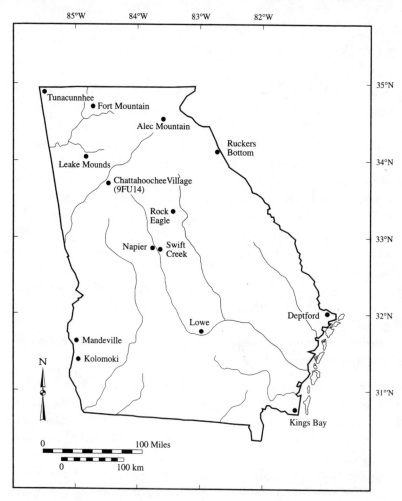

Map 4. Some Woodland sites in Georgia

site is found to be stratified, the sequence of pottery types can be worked out from the earliest to the latest. In just this manner, archaeologists in the late nineteenth and early twentieth centuries established sequences of pottery types in the Southeast.

Everyday life for the people in what is now Georgia actually changed little from Archaic to Woodland times. With the establishment of an essentially modern climate in the Southeast, the increased rainfall led to higher water levels in the rivers, which probably accounts for the virtual disappearance of freshwater shellfish from the diet. The shell heaps so prominent in the Middle and Late Archaic ceased to grow as the people shifted subsistence activities away from this increasingly unattainable resource. In fact, for groups who lived far from the larger rivers, life changed hardly at all.

Seasonal hunting and gathering continued as it had. Groups who lived along the Georgia coast mined the rich marine and coastal resources and hunted and gathered in the inland forest. Those in the Coastal Plain, Piedmont, and mountains followed the seasonal cycle, hunting and gathering as natural foods became available in different environmental zones or niches in their territory. Some groups probably continued to grow cultivated plants, an activity that began in the Late Archaic. However, from all indications these plants were still unimportant in the overall diet of the people, and they could have gotten along without them.

Early Woodland (1000 B.C.–A.D. 1)

The Early Woodland Period in the mountains and Piedmont of Georgia is marked by the appearance in the archaeological record of grit-tempered pottery. Decorated with a fabric-wrapped paddle or stick, this is called Dunlap fabric-marked pottery. It is part of what one archaeologist originally identified as the "Kellog focus," a prehistoric cultural complex that included fabric-marked pottery, round-house structures, and numerous cylindrical or bell-shaped storage pits that contained the remains of acorns, walnuts, and hickory nuts. Since no remains of cultivated plants were found in any of these storage pits, it was concluded that these people were not growing domesticated plants but were strictly hunters and gatherers.

Other traits of this cultural phase identified by archaeologists include medium-sized triangular projectile points, large stone-lined cooking pits, and flexed burials in circular or semi-circular pits. Sites are typically on

Fig. 4.1. Dunlap fabric-marked pottery (from a private collection; photo by David Price)

the floodplain of rivers and sometimes cover an acre or more. Thick middens have been found at some sites of this period, and the larger cooking pits are up to three feet deep.

That the remains of this culture are found primarily in the mountains and Piedmont has led archaeologists to suggest that they represented an adaptation to life in the deciduous forest that covered this area. One reason for this belief is that fabric-marked pottery is not much in evidence below the Fall Line, although it is present on some sites, especially along the Chattahoochee River. A few radiocarbon dates from excavated sites indicate approximately 800–200 B.C. for the Kellog Phase.

The Kellog Phase is followed in the archaeological record by the appearance of simple-stamped pottery and Cartersville check-stamped pottery, thought to represent a period about 300–100 B.C. Cartersville check-stamped pottery is the inland equivalent of the Deptford check-stamped pottery of the coastal region.

Along Georgia's coast, the Woodland Period is marked by the appearance of traits associated with the Refuge Phase. Named for a site excavated on the South Carolina side of the Savannah River, Refuge ceramics bear punctated, simple-stamped, dentate-stamped, and (later) check-stamped decorations. Archaeologists believe that Refuge pottery evolved from the St. Simons fiber-tempered ceramics (now considered to be the same as Stalling's Island ceramics), for there is apparently a continuity of designs, but Refuge ceramics are characterized by a coarse, gritty paste, and vessels were made by the rope-coil method rather than by molding. These ceramics are found over a wide area of southeastern Georgia. Sites inland from the coast mostly lie on higher ground and show no evidence

Fig. 4.2. Projectile points of the Woodland Period (from a private collection; photo by David Price)

Fig. 4.3. Cartersville check-stamped pottery and simple-stamped pottery (from a private collection; photo by David Price)

of long-term occupation. Along the coast itself, Refuge ceramics are often found on top of middens of the St. Simons Phase located in the marsh.

Excavations on St. Simons Island have revealed considerably more information on the Refuge Phase of the Early Woodland. Discovered under some three feet of marsh sediments was a Refuge occupation layer. No shellfish were present in the layer. Pottery included Refuge plain and Refuge simple-stamped, and radiocarbon dates place the occupation at about 800 B.C. Animal remains from the midden include deer, small mammals, turtles, and alligator. The presence of stone tools and debris suggests that hunting grew more important at this time. If these people did eat shellfish, the absence of remains can be explained by fluctuations in sea level. Geological studies demonstrate that there was a drop in sea level of six to twelve feet around 1000 B.C., and any evidence of the use of shellfish from the coastal marsh would be farther east, toward what was then the coast. Such middens would now be either submerged or buried beneath dunes or marsh. By about 400 B.C., the sea reached close to its present level.

Beginning about 500 B.C., a new ceramic style appeared along the Georgia coast. It is referred to as Deptford, and sites that belong to this tradition have received much attention from archaeologists in the past few years. Pottery associated with the Early Deptford Phase is typically decorated with check-stamped, cord-marked, or simple-stamped designs. Deptford sites are known to occur in the live oak forest on the mainland and on the barrier islands adjacent to saltwater marsh, as well as in the coastal plain, especially adjacent to the coast. As noted earlier, the north Georgia equivalent pottery type is called Cartersville check-stamped. Archaeologists who have studied the Deptford Phase along the coast believe that the sites demonstrate an orientation toward exploiting the varied food sources associated with the saltwater marsh. Inland sites, which are small, likely reflect hunting and gathering stations where temporary camps were established. Settlements along the coast and on the barrier islands were larger and more permanent. In fact, excavations on Cumberland Island show that sites associated with the Early Deptford occupation were composed of a row of five to ten house structures along the edge of the marsh. Some structures were constructed rather well, with vertical wall posts anchored in shell-filled trenches. Evidently, open-sided structures similar to the modern Seminole chickee were also present. Abundant coastal and marsh resources encouraged permanent or semi-permanent village life. Among the faunal remains recovered from Deptford contexts on Cumberland Island were opossum, white-tailed deer, bear, raccoon, turtle, rabbit, alligator, shark, catfish, drum, snapper, mullet, freshwater mussel, oyster, clam, whelk, and periwinkle.

Excavations on St. Catherines Island demonstrate that several small mounds constructed of sand date to the Refuge-Deptford occupation. These sites were used for burials, and the central tomb at the McLeod Mound contained oyster and clam shells that dated to 450 B.C. Burials in these sand mounds contained few artifacts, but radiocarbon dates suggest their use and construction date to 1500 B.C. to A.D. 600 (see Thomas and Larsen 1979). Why these people began to construct such burial mounds has been the subject of speculation among archaeologists working on the Georgia coast. It is believed that many more such mounds exist, but because of their small size they are easy to overlook.

Middle Woodland (A.D. 1–500)

Archaeologists believe that the more permanent village life made possible by exploiting abundant resources set the stage for the growth of population and social complexity evident during the Middle Woodland. During this time, cultures in Georgia and other parts of the Southeast came under the influence of the Ohio Valley's Hopewell culture, named for the family whose farm in Ohio contained numerous mounds and earthworks associated with this culture. Since the people left no writing, we do not know their tribal identity, yet what the archaeological record has revealed is nothing short of amazing.

About the time of Christ or slightly earlier, people living in the Ohio Valley developed or elaborated upon what must have been a vigorous ceremonial complex. It involved the construction of earthworks, sometimes in precise geometric shapes, sometimes in the form of animal or bird effigies. Archaeologists have traditionally assigned the serpent mound in Ohio to the Hopewell culture, but recent excavations indicate that it was built later. The Hopewell people also constructed mounds of earth over log tombs of the leaders of their society. Buried with them were exotic goods originating at great distances from the Hopewell heartland. Obsidian was obtained from what is now Yellowstone National Park in Wyoming, teeth and claws from grizzly bears from the western plains, copper from the Great Lakes region, mica from the Southern Appalachians, and seashells from the Gulf Coast. These were sometimes made into beautiful objects: sheets of mica, for example, were cut into the shape of human hands or bird claws. A distinctive array of artifacts typified the mound burials and included copper-covered panpipes, small human effigies of clay, platform pipes, and copper-covered wooden earspools. Possibly due to the trade network established to obtain exotic goods, Hopewell influences begin to appear in the archaeological record in Georgia during Middle Woodland times.

A distinctive pottery style of the Middle Woodland in Georgia is named Swift Creek for a site on a tributary of the Ocmulgee River near Macon. This pottery is identified by its ornate and well-executed decoration applied by pressing a carved wooden paddle into the clay before firing. Archaeologists have studied Swift Creek designs and attempted some reconstructions, using whole or fragmentary pottery vessels. Many of the designs are curvilinear, and some are believed to represent insects, birds, snakes, flowers, and human masks, all highly stylized (see Snow 1975, 1977). One archaeologist describes early Swift Creek complicated-stamped pottery as "characterized by curvilinear motifs (circles, spirals, teardrops), conoidal vessel shape, small tetrapodal supports, and notched or scalloped rims" (B. Smith 1977:66). Swift Creek pottery is most common in southern Georgia but is also present in the Piedmont and moun-

Fig. 4.4. Swift Creek complicated-stamped pottery (courtesy Laboratory of Archaeology, Department of Anthropology, University of Georgia; photo by David Price)

tains, as well as in other states. One large Hopewell site in southern Indiana contains Swift Creek pottery identical to the Georgia ware, a situation that led one archaeologist to suggest the possibility that a colony of artisans from southern Georgia might have lived at this major ceremonial center. In Georgia, one of the earliest sites at which Swift Creek ceramics have been found associated with Hopewell manifestations is the Mandeville site on the Chattahoochee River in Clay County.

The Mandeville site—two mounds and a village area—was the scene of excavations in the late 1950s and early 1960s. Mound A was a flat-topped mound some 14 feet high and measuring 240 by 170 feet. The top layer had been added by people of a later period (the Mississippian) and thus did not date to the period under consideration here. Mound B was a conical mound 18 feet high and 100 feet in diameter. Although archaeologists then believed the earliest level of Mound A could be assigned to a Late Deptford occupation, subsequent study has placed it in the Early Swift Creek Phase. Radiocarbon dates indicate that this Swift Creek occupation began about A.D. 140 and that construction of both mounds had begun by A.D. 250.

Mound A consisted of five layers, the last dating to about 500 years later than the Middle Woodland occupation. In the earliest two levels of mound construction, plain, simple-stamped, and check-stamped pottery dominated, with complicated-stamped wares present and more frequent over time. From the earliest level, Mound A had been a flat-topped rectangular structure. Archaeologists found little or no evidence of any type of structure on the mound summit in the Middle Woodland components, leading to the conclusion that if a structure had topped the mound, it was temporary and insubstantial.

Excavation of Mound B, a burial mound, revealed several Hopewell items. A female figurine and its archaeological context are described by the archaeologists who found them: "It is 3½ inches high and was found in a pit (Feature 10). . . . The upper part of this pit had been subjected to much heat and a large mass of charcoal was still present. The figurine was at the base of this depression lying face down and adjacent to a fragment of galena. It is a representation of a woman bent slightly forward at the waist with the hands at the side with fingers extended. Though the hands were detailed even to the knuckles, the left thumb had not been modeled. The skirt, portions of the feet, hairline and armbands are painted red, while the hair and portions of the back are painted black. Her hair is

Fig. 4.5. Hopewellian pipes from the Tunacunnhee site, Dade County (courtesy Laboratory of Archaeology, Department of Anthropology, University of Georgia)

parted to the left, tapers down the back, and is squared off just above the waist" (Kellar et al. 1962:351).

Other Hopewellian artifacts included copper-covered earspools, copper-covered panpipes, clay platform pipes, cut mica, and prismatic flint blades, four of the last identified as having originated at Flint Ridge, Ohio.

During Middle Woodland times, peoples living in southwest Georgia came under the influence of cultures from the northwest Florida Gulf Coast. Ties with the Santa Rosa–Swift Creek culture of Florida are apparent at the Mandeville site, and the influence of Florida cultures on southwest Georgia continues into the Late Woodland Period.

Another Hopewell site in Georgia is the Tunacunnhee site in Dade County, in the northwest part of the state, excavated by the University of Georgia beginning in 1973. The site consisted of a group of eight mounds on Lookout Creek near the western slope of Lookout Mountain. The largest, Mound A, covered an area of 1,500 square feet and was constructed of limestone slabs and earth. Excavation revealed that four nearby mounds were of modern origin (farmers' rock piles), but a hundred feet southwest of Mound A were three circular earth mounds capped with limestone. Mound C covered an area of 850 square feet, Mound D 113 square feet, and Mound E about 500 square feet.

Excavations into Mound A revealed a central burial pit partly surrounded by a ring of red clay from one to four feet wide and approximately one foot thick. The pit contained fragments of bone, some burned, and a portion of a copper earspool. In other areas of the mound, four additional burials were encountered, most of them poorly preserved. A piece of octagon-shaped mica and a small copper band were found with one of these burials.

Mound C was a circular earth mound with a cap or mantle of limestone rocks. A central burial pit contained a large mica disc and the remains of what was evidently a woven bag, since the copper objects it contained had impressions of the weaving preserved on them. The bag had contained a rectangular copper plate, two sets of copper earspools, a copper awl or pin, and some thirty small beads made from the vertebrae

Fig. 4.6. View of the excavations by the University of Georgia at the Tunacunnhee site (courtesy Laboratory of Archaeology, Department of Anthropology, University of Georgia)

of a small animal. The fabric remains yielded a radiocarbon date of about A.D. 150. Other artifacts associated with the fabric bag included shark vertebrae, two human mandibles, two drilled shark teeth, a drilled bear canine, and a black chert knife or scraper. Placed on top of the fill of this pit was the skeleton of an adult male. A large mica cutout in the shape of a claw or hook was found on top of the skull, placed so that the claw circled the right eye. As in Mound A, a ring of red clay encircled the central burial pit. Several other burials containing typical Hopewellian artifacts were recovered from other areas of Mound C.

While the Mandeville and Tunacunnhee sites are perhaps the best known and most extensively investigated Hopewellian sites in Georgia, there are others that have received some attention from archaeologists. These include the Leake Mound in Bartow County (see Price 1994; Pluck-hahn 1998) and the Little River mounds and village in Morgan County (see Williams and Shapiro 1990). Other types of sites believed to be associated with Hopewell influence in the area are various stone structures, circles, mounds, and formations. Chief among these is the Rock Eagle effigy near Eatonton, in Putnam County. Measuring 120 feet from wing tip to wing tip, and 102 feet from head to tail, the effigy is constructed of quartzite stones of varying sizes. Whether the bird in fact represented an eagle or some other bird is not known. In an attempt to learn more about this effigy, archaeologist A. R. Kelly of the University of Georgia excavated its breast area during the 1950s. In a class that he taught in 1967, he recalled that in moving the stones, a single quartz projectile point was found. When the original ground surface underneath the effigy was reached, the remains of a single cremated human burial were found. No burial objects were present, and Kelly concluded that the projectile point and the burial may or may not have had any connection with the construction of the effigy. At least one other similar effigy is known in that same area.

Elsewhere in Georgia, numerous stone mounds, walls, and other stone structures are believed to be associated with the Hopewell culture, although their purpose or function remains a mystery. One of the best known stands atop Fort Mountain in Murray County, northwest Georgia. This stone wall varies in height from 3 to 10 feet, is about 4½ feet wide, and extends for about 928 feet near the summit of Fort Mountain. Test excavations into the wall revealed no artifacts, and the archaeologist investigating the structure concluded that it could not have been built for

Fig. 4.7. Stone wall on Fort Mountain, Murray County (courtesy Georgia Department of Natural Resources)

defense purposes, for no source of water lies within the enclosure and people inside the circle would in some spots be completely vulnerable to anyone on the outside. Similar walls are known to have been constructed on Stone Mountain, Sand Mountain, Rocky Face Mountain (near Dalton), Brown's Mount (Bibb County), Ladd Mountain (Bartow County), and other locations, but most have been destroyed. The wall on Stone Mountain, for instance, was dismantled in the early twentieth century by road crews who used the stones as road fill. In the late 1950s, an archaeologist who conducted excavations at a stone circle on Alec Mountain in Habersham County found no artifacts.

Scattered throughout the Piedmont and mountains of Georgia are rock piles, thought by some to be Indian burial sites. One must be extremely careful in identifying these features as Indian burial mounds, or even of Indian origin. Some rock piles investigated by archaeologists were found to contain charcoal and pottery fragments that could be identified as Middle Woodland. However, most yielded no artifacts at all or artifacts of recent vintage, such as broken glass, indicating that they are the result of a farmer trying to clear his field of rocks. We do know that some rock piles are prehistoric, so all such features need to be brought to the attention of archaeologists. Widespread development, particularly in the region surrounding Atlanta, has brought about the destruction of numerous sites and the discovery of others, including stone mounds and rock piles.

Why do archaeologists believe these structures are associated with the Hopewell culture when artifacts linking them to this time period are rarely if ever found in association? The answer is that similar structures in other states have sometimes yielded artifacts or radiocarbon dates placing them in the Hopewell era. The Old Stone Fort in north-central Tennessee is an example: A hearth at the base of the wall yielded a radiocarbon date of about A.D. 400. Still, why so much energy and time would be expended to construct these features remains one of many mysteries surrounding the Hopewell culture.

Not all Middle Woodland peoples participated in this ceremonialism, for evidence of Hopewell influence is not seen throughout the state. One large and important site of this period where few if any Hopewellian manifestations were apparent lay on the Chattahoochee River just southwest of Atlanta. It was here that industrial development in the late 1960s led to the discovery of a village consisting of the remains of some thirty dwellings. The structures were round or oval, about fifteen feet in diameter, and each had at the center a well-preserved hearth or cooking pit filled with fire-cracked rock, ash, and charcoal. A radiocarbon test on material from one of these pits yielded a date of about A.D. 214. This and the ceramics recovered from the site place the village in the Cartersville Phase of the Middle Woodland. It is interesting that the houses had depressed or saucer-shaped floors. A similar village site from the same period was excavated on the grounds of Pebblebrook High School just north of Atlanta. No burials were found at either site, but abundant floral and faunal remains enabled archaeologists to draw some rather startling conclusions.

It was apparent that settled village life had been accomplished without agriculture. Earlier, some anthropologists had assumed that in order for permanent villages to exist, there had to be the social stability that comes from an agriculture-based economy. However, in the Piedmont of Georgia, the environment was so rich in natural foods that settled village life was possible even without agriculture. The flotation technique for recovering small-scale remains was used at the village site southwest of Atlanta, and the dirt scraped from the house floors yielded an abundance of seeds, bones, and other evidence of environmental exploitation. Archaeologists identified fish, turtle, bird, and other remains, as well as various seeds and nuts. But the lack of remains of squash, maize, or other familiar cultivated plants indicates the unimportance of domesticated plants for people living in this part of Georgia in Middle Woodland times. While such plants were being grown in some areas, they still appear to have been of minimal importance in the overall diet and were simply additional sources of food.

One of the most thoroughly investigated Middle Woodland sites in north Georgia is the Hickory Log site in Cherokee County. Pottery associated with the Middle Woodland occupation at this multicomponent site included Cartersville simple-stamped, Cartersville check-stamped, and Swift Creek complicated-stamped wares. The remains of twelve structures were encountered, along with roasting pits, storage pits, hearths, and a few human burials. Plant remains recovered from Middle Woodland contexts show that hickory nuts and acorns were heavily used, along with walnuts and hazelnuts. Maize was present, as in the Ice House Bottom site in Tennessee, where a date of a.d. 175 was obtained. This date is consistent with dates from the Hickory Log site (about a.d. 250–450), demonstrating that maize (corn) was being grown in the Southeast in Middle Woodland times. Hickory Log also yielded remains of squash and maygrass, along with numerous remains of wild plants gathered from the surrounding forest and river bottoms (see Garrow 2000). The findings at Hickory Log, consistent with archaeological discoveries at other sites in the region, indicate a primary reliance on hunting and gathering, with cultivated plants contributing additional food.

So our villagers on the upper Chattahoochee must have been backward country cousins of their relatives down river. If they lacked the metropolitan and civilized glamour of the early mound builders, they still had improved the Archaic techniques of getting and preparing food to the point that they could live in permanent, settled villages. Apparently, they accomplished this without the "economic surplus" of developed agriculture, once thought to be essential for the development of a sedentary population. (Kelly 1973: 37)

Late Woodland (A.D. 500–1000)

The Late Woodland in Georgia is identified by distinctive pottery decorations used at this time and by evidence of increasing influence in some areas from culture centers outside the state, including the Santa Rosa–Swift Creek culture of the Florida Gulf Coast. This in turn was a Hopewell-derived culture. One of the largest and most impressive sites of this manifestation is the Kolomoki site in Early County, in southwest Georgia. Radiocarbon dates place the primary period of village occupation and mound construction at this site at A.D. 300–500 (Middle Woodland). The building of mounds and associated elaborate burials ceased after about A.D. 750, so the Kolomoki manifestation apparently evolved in the Middle Woodland and persisted well into Late Woodland times.

The Kolomoki site covers some 300 acres near a small tributary of the Chattahoochee River. The village area forms an arc around a large mound, a plaza area, and several smaller mounds. The large mound that dominates the site, 56 feet in height and 325 by 200 feet at its base, received only minor attention when the site was excavated in the mid-twentieth century. The limited excavations carried out on this mound (Mound A) revealed that it had been capped by a layer of red clay that overlay a hard-

Fig. 4.8. A mound at the Kolomoki site, Early County (courtesy Georgia Department of Natural Resources)

packed surface of white clay, interpreted as representing the cap on the last fully buried mound-construction stage.

Excavation of Mound D, a tumulus 20 feet high and 100 feet in diameter, revealed that it was a burial mound. Five individuals were found in log-lined graves and another male in a rock slab and log grave nearby, along with other remains of burials or cremations (see inset). Mound E, smaller than Mound D, apparently served a similar function. At the base of a central pit were the cremated remains of an individual who had been interred with a large number of shell beads and two copper ornaments with pearls in their centers. Two other bodies had been placed on the sloping upper portion of this pit; all were covered in earth, and the whole capped in rocks. A single human skull with a copper-covered wooden ornament was placed on top of this mound. A mass of fifty-four complete

---

The first step was clearing an area about fifty feet in diameter of all debris, including midden. Five individuals, slightly flexed at the knees accompanied by a few beads, were interred here in log lined graves. As their graves were being filled, eight large logs were held in a vertical position. The earth mounding over the graves, plus midden from the area which had been scraped aside, was used to support these logs in the upright position. The resultant primary mound was then covered with rocks. After the scaffold was complete, but before any more construction took place, one male was buried in a rock slab and log grave adjacent to the southern edge of the scaffold. After the earth was piled into and over his grave, several individuals or parts of them were cremated on top of the earth. A square framework of poles, believed to have been a litter, was then placed on top of the cremated remains. Two more individuals, the only two definitely female bodies in the mound, were placed in two more rock slab and log tombs, side by side, in front of the scaffold. In all three cases, no offerings were placed in the graves, except for occasional conch beads which appear to have been ornaments in place on the bodies at the time of burial rather than offerings *per se*. It may be noted that a definite relationship is implied between the male and the two females in terms of shared use of the scaffolding and the common grave type. (Sears 1956: 11–12)

pottery vessels was then placed on the ground surface just to the east of this mound. Finally, the initial mound and the pottery were covered in a layer of red clay (see Sears 1956).

The Kolomoki site is particularly notable for the effigy pottery found there in mortuary contexts, hollow clay vessels with precut holes and perforations as part of the decoration. Some were free standing, modeled in the shape of a deer or bird, while others were pedestaled and usually represented a duck, owl, or raptor. Others, in the shape of functional vessels, had been modified by the addition of an effigy of an animal or bird head. Since most such vessels could have had no utilitarian purpose, they are regarded by archaeologists as ceremonial in nature. Utilitarian pottery recovered at this site has been identified as Late Swift Creek, Weeden Island, and some other types, such as Lamar, associated with later occupations of the site.

Fig. 4.9. Effigy jar from the Kolomoki site (courtesy Georgia Department of Natural Resources)

Along the Georgia coast, the Late Woodland is evidenced by cultural changes manifested in new pottery styles, the cessation of mound building, and an increasing shift toward exploiting food sources in the marshes. This is the Kelvin Phase of the Late Woodland and applies to the coastal area south of the mouth of the Altamaha River. Although mound building ceased, population growth is evidenced by the larger villages on the coastal islands. The excavation of a Kelvin Phase house on St. Simons Island revealed a rather large structure, its floor littered with fish remains, and three large hearths marked by ash mounds. At least six large Kelvin Phase sites are known on St. Simons Island, and evidence indicates intensive exploitation of the marsh environment. One archaeologist with extensive knowledge of coastal prehistory speculates that the exploitation of the marshes through hunting and gathering was supplemented by some agriculture, as was the case in early historic times on the coast (see Cook 1977).

Pottery of the Kelvin Phase is either plain or complicated-stamped, with the designs of the latter resembling Swift Creek types. Some vessels have a crudely modeled rim similar to some Swift Creek vessels. The Kelvin Phase is believed to date to A.D. 600–800.

On the upper Georgia coast, the Late Woodland is characterized by the appearance of the Wilmington ceramic complex. The clay-tempered cord-

Fig. 4.10. Cord-marked pottery (from a private collection; photo by David Price)

marked pottery appeared in the archaeological record about A.D. 700 and remained in use until about A.D. 1000. Some archaeologists believe that the appearance of Wilmington ceramics might indicate a movement of people from the river valleys of the Coastal Plain to the coast and barrier islands. Along the Ocmulgee River below the Fall Line, cord-marked pottery is present, but it differs from the pottery of the coast during this time, particularly in the folded rims of the Ocmulgee cord-marked pottery. What relationship this tradition has to the coastal cord-marked pottery remains unclear.

In northern Georgia, the Late Woodland Period saw the introduction of Swift Creek pottery, an event generally thought to have occurred after A.D. 400. As Swift Creek complicated-stamped pottery gained in popularity, Cartersville check-stamped decoration declined and disappeared. However, there is evidence that in some areas simple-stamped and plain pottery continued to be used in the Late Woodland. The Ruckers Bottom site and another site on the upper Savannah River had simple-stamped and plain pottery associated with features dated to A.D. 800 and 1000. Swift Creek complicated-stamped pottery and Napier complicated-stamped pottery (a type that appears in the Late Swift Creek Phase in middle Georgia) are both present in the Late Woodland of north Georgia. However, sites bearing these pottery types are not as common as those of the earlier Cartersville Phase, and they appear to be absent altogether in the Ridge and Valley province of northwest Georgia and adjacent portions of the western Piedmont.

Other artifacts associated with the Late Woodland in northern Georgia are small, stemmed, side-notched projectile points made of chert or quartz, as well as grinding stones and hammerstones.

Fig. 4.11. Napier complicated-stamped pottery (from a private collection; photo by David Price)

Evidence of subsistence during the Late Woodland of northern Georgia is mostly inferential, for few sites of this period have been excavated. The limited amount of information that we have indicates a continuation of the hunting-and-gathering pattern of earlier times with the addition of cultivated plants. The earliest secure date so far for corn (maize) in Georgia is from the Rush site in the northwest, which yielded a date of A.D. 660. A Late Woodland component at a site in South Carolina just across the Savannah River yielded remains of sunflower and squash or gourd. Still, it appears that although domesticated plants were being grown by Woodland peoples in some areas, they played a minor role in their overall diet. This was to change drastically in the next time period, the Mississippian.

Conclusion

In looking back over the Woodland Period, it is well to remember, as anthropologists know, that it is inaccurate to state that a culture has remained unchanged for thousands of years. Change is constant, even though it cannot always be detected in the archaeological record. New ideas, new ways of doing things, and new customs arise, a good thing to keep in mind in looking back over the Woodland Period. Very little of the cultural inventory remains, so archaeologists are once again dependent on physical artifacts as a basis for interpreting the past. It is also well to remember that the peoples who lived in the various regions of Georgia during the Woodland did not live in isolation. Travel and trade occurred, and along with them ideas spread. Some artifacts are good indicators of the spread of ideas or even of population movements. One such artifact is pottery.

Pottery was first made during the Late Archaic, its technology and decoration evolving over time. The pottery of the Late Archaic was made by molding clay tempered with vegetal fiber into a vessel shape and often decorating the completed vessel by the stab-and-drag technique. With the Woodland Period, however, the rope-coil method was introduced, the clay was tempered with grit or sand, and decorations consisted of check-stamped, fabric-marked, cord-marked, and complicated-stamped designs. Through time, some decorative techniques were abandoned and new ones appeared. Other changes in technology appear in projectile-point types, which are smaller than those of the Late Archaic. A major technological innovation was the introduction of the bow and arrow, thought to have occurred between A.D. 700 and 800. Much more efficient than the atl-atl, this weapon apparently replaced it throughout the region.

In subsistence, the Woodland Period witnessed little change from the Archaic. Hunting, fishing, and gathering continued to be the way of life in all regions of Georgia, with plants cultivated in some areas. Corn (maize) was introduced, but it and the other cultivated plants apparently served only as additional, and perhaps exotic, sources of food and were unimportant in the overall economy. The growing of cultivated plants was evidently made possible by the abundance of natural foods, which made it possible for people to remain in one place for an extended period of time. Abundant food and at least semi-permanent settlements might have fostered population growth and increasing social complexity.

Some anthropologists believe, however, that population growth led to an increasing scarcity of food, leading to competition and promoting group solidarity. These in turn could have led to increasing social complexity and the appearance of ranked societies. Whatever the origin, the growth of socially ranked societies is believed to be indicated by the construction of burial mounds over the graves or tombs of the elite. Such graves sometimes contain exotic furnishings that probably indicate the high social status of the individuals buried there. Some archaeologists believe that the increase in population and social complexity underlie the appearance of the much more sophisticated societies in the next time period, the Mississippian.

Suggestions for Further Reading

Caldwell, Joseph R. 1958. *Trend and Tradition in the Prehistory of the Eastern United States.* American Anthropological Association Memoir 88.

Gresham, Thomas H. 1990. "Historic Patterns of Rock Piling and the Rock Pile Problem." *Early Georgia* 18, 1–2: 1–40.

Jefferies, Richard W. 1976. *The Tunacunnhee Site: Evidence of Hopewell Interaction in Northwest Georgia.* Anthropological Papers of the University of Georgia 1. Athens: University of Georgia Press.

Sears, William H. 1956. *Excavations at Kolomoki: Final Report.* University of Georgia Series in Anthropology 5. Athens: University of Georgia Press.

Smith, Philip E. 1962. *Aboriginal Stone Constructions in the Southern Piedmont.* Report 4, pt. 2. Athens: University of Georgia Laboratory of Archaeology.

Wauchope, Robert. 1966. *Archaeological Survey of Northern Georgia.* Memoirs of the Society for American Archaeology 21. Salt Lake City: Society for American Archaeology.

5

The Mississippian Period, A.D. 1000–1500

The young warrior walked down the path toward the river, his thoughts on the project at hand. He had been chosen along with a few others to represent his clan in an important task made all the more special by the infrequency of its occurrence. As he approached the river, he smelled the rich, dank weeds growing along the bank. Heating up in the sun, they gave off the smell of summer's fullness, for it was late in the season. In the woods across the river, a pileated woodpecker noisily announced its presence, while cicadas sang in the trees that leaned over the water. At the river, several men were quarrying dark-gray clay from the bank. It was this clay that the warrior and the others were carrying in baskets all the way back to the mound in the center of their town.

The clay was being used to create a new layer on the mound, making it even bigger and more impressive. The fresh gray clay would contrast sharply with the bright-red clay that would form the steps to the summit, where a new temple was to be erected. The mound and its temple were a source of pride, as they represented the power and prestige of the village chief, his lineage, the clans, and in fact all the people who belonged to this town. They also evoked thoughts of the town's heritage, the greatness of the ancestors, the accomplishments of past leaders. The warrior anticipated with eagerness the great ceremony of dedication to be held when the mound and its new temple were finished. It was an event that happened maybe once in a lifetime, and he was fortunate to be playing a role in this great occasion.

Early Mississippian (A.D. 1000–1200)

During the century or so preceding 1000 A.D., noticeable changes were taking place among the people living in what is now Georgia. One might say that a way of life was ending and another beginning. The hunting, fishing, and gathering activities basic to the patterns of life during the Woodland Period would become of secondary importance. Agriculture, so insignificant in the Woodland, would provide the primary source of food in the Mississippian. Along with the agricultural way of life came a ceremonial system or religion that came to be practiced by people throughout the Southeast. This time period takes its name from the Mississippi Valley, where archaeologists first identified this characteristic way of life. The ceremonial system consisted of the construction of flat-topped temple mounds made of earth, ceremonial earth lodges, and the use of distinctive paraphernalia and art motifs. We have glimpses of this ceremonialism in descriptions left by the first Europeans to enter the Southeast during the sixteenth century, whose intrusion forecast the end of Mississippian society.

Archaeologists now believe that the earliest expression of Mississippian traits in northern Georgia occurred in a transitional phase of the Late Woodland, the Woodstock culture, dated to A.D. 900–1000. As in the earlier Woodland, pottery is one of the most useful characteristics in identifying this cultural expression. The style of decoration is believed to have developed out of the north Georgia Swift Creek and Napier styles. Woodstock ceramic decoration is primarily complicated-stamping, and design elements are herringbone, concentric-circle, line-block, diamond, and oval patterns. Few Woodstock sites have been excavated, but those that have been investigated reveal some interesting characteristics, indicating that this culture may represent the transition from the Woodland way of life to the Mississippian.

Perhaps the best known Woodstock site is the one excavated in 1950 by Joseph Caldwell. It was on the Etowah River in Cherokee County and was investigated hurriedly just before it was submerged because of the Allatoona dam. Caldwell discovered a palisade consisting of a double row of posts, with two square towers and one round tower, all surrounded by a shallow ditch. Such fortifications are typical of Mississippian sites. Also, at the Summerour site on the Chattahoochee River in Forsyth County, Caldwell excavated a mound that he assigned to the Woodstock culture on the basis of the pottery (Swift Creek, Napier, and Woodstock). The

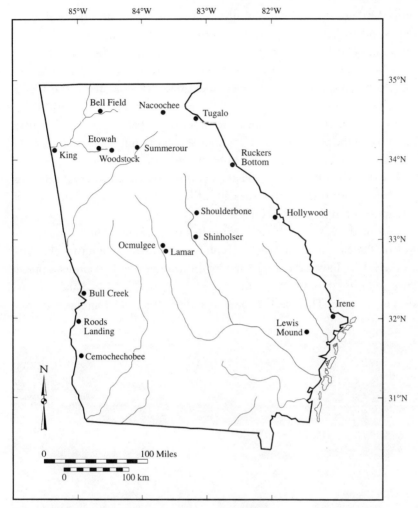

Map 5. Selected Mississippian sites in Georgia

mound contained the remains of a structure on its summit, with wall trenches characteristic of Mississippian structures.

Woodstock sites seem to be concentrated in the upper Piedmont, but they also occur in northwest Georgia's Ridge and Valley province and in the Blue Ridge Mountains. They apparently do not extend below the Fall Line. Sites occur along streams, particularly the upper Chattahoochee and Etowah Rivers, often on old alluvial terraces above the floodplain. Upland sites are thought to represent seasonal hunting-and-gathering stations. Little evidence of agriculture has been found in sites that belong to the Woodstock culture. Only two kernels of corn (maize) were found at the Stamp Creek site (Bartow County), and a feature at the Lum Moss site (Gordon County) yielded corn and a radiocarbon date of A.D. 990, but this feature could not be positively identified as belonging to the Woodstock occupation. Small amounts of corn were found at two other sites (Potts Tract in Murray County and Whitehead Farm in Floyd County), but most of the plant remains consisted of hickory nut, walnut, and acorn, indicating a primary reliance on hunting and gathering. The conclusion of archaeologists is that the Woodstock peoples practiced a very limited agriculture. Corn (maize) was present, at least in some areas, but was still unimportant in the overall diet.

One of the earliest Mississippian sites in Georgia is the Ocmulgee or Macon Plateau site near Macon (Bibb County). Archaeologists who have worked there have been impressed by the apparent rather sudden appearance and growth of this site and by how different it is from contemporary sites in the area. This has led some to suggest that the Ocmulgee site rep-

Fig. 5.1. View of mounds at the Ocmulgee (Macon Plateau) site, Bibb County (courtesy National Park Service)

resents the intrusion into the area of a new group of people who followed the Mississippian way of life. Actually, there are two centers of what some have called the Macon Plateau culture, the Ocmulgee site itself and the Brown's Mount site a few miles away. Radiocarbon dates indicate occupation of both sites at about A.D. 1000. The Ocmulgee site is the larger and more impressive of the two.

The Ocmulgee site is situated on a relatively flat extension of uplands that on its eastern side overlooks the Ocmulgee River. In places, a rather steep escarpment borders the floodplain. On these uplands, the Early Mississippian inhabitants at Ocmulgee built a major ceremonial center of six temple mounds and several earth lodges, one of which has been reconstructed. The largest of the mounds, some fifty feet high, stands on the edge of the escarpment overlooking the river. This aspect makes it appear to be even larger. Excavations here in the 1930s revealed that the ground surface had been leveled prior to construction of the mound and that the mound had been built in at least five stages, each consisting of a layer of sand fill capped by a layer of clay. Named Mound A, this structure has not been completely excavated.

Most of Mound B, located nearby, was removed during railroad construction in the 1800s. Excavations in the 1930s in the remnant revealed that this mound had been built in four stages. Mound C, named the Funeral Mound, had also been partially destroyed by railroad construction, and excavations demonstrated that it had been built in seven stages. Burials were encountered, and because of their location in or near the mound and their exotic grave furnishings, archaeologists conclude that these are the burials of the social elite, probably members of the families of the social/religious leaders. One such grave in this mound consisted of a pit eight feet long that contained poorly preserved skeletal remains but astonishing grave furnishings: two copper plates and two copper-covered cut puma jaws, along with fragments of cane matting and a piece of twisted cord preserved by the copper salts. Excavations also revealed that Mound C contained a stairway from the base to the summit of the first mound stage. These steps were made of brilliant red clay placed on the blue-gray clay of the mound cap, and the archaeologists noted that they were heavily worn by the trodding of feet.

One of the most surprising and unique finds at the Ocmulgee site was the ceremonial earth lodge. When workers began excavating a small mound about three feet high and seventy feet in diameter, they encountered a red clay wall surrounding an inner area forty-two feet across with a circular fire basin near its center. Further excavations revealed an entrance passageway twenty-six feet long and two feet wide lined with the charred remains of split-cane matting. In the spring of 1967, I was enrolled in an archaeology class taught by A. R. Kelly at the University of Georgia. Nearing retirement, he decided to take the class on a field trip to the Ocmulgee site, where he had supervised excavations more than thirty years earlier. As we inspected the reconstructed ceremonial earth lodge, he remarked that evidence encountered in the entrance passageway indicated that it was a very low edifice, probably requiring that one enter on hands and knees.

Inside this structure, directly opposite the entrance was a large, clay, eagle-shaped platform. On either side of this platform and extending around the wall to the entrance was a row of seats modeled in clay, with a receptacle in front of each. The roof of this unique structure had been supported by four huge oak posts, the charred remains of which were intact. Charred timbers and fragments of cane matting littered the floor. It was evident that the earth-covered structure had burned and collapsed,

Fig. 5.2. Museum diorama of a ceremony in the earth lodge (courtesy National Park Service)

the charred timbers and overlying layer of earth creating a protective layer over the floor of the chamber. This structure has been restored; visitors to Ocmulgee National Monument can enter and view the original floor just as the archaeologists found it.

Another unique find was made when Mound D, the Cornfield Mound, was excavated. This small mound was found to have been constructed directly on a cornfield. The corn rows, and even a path through the field, could be seen.

Of the remaining mounds at the Ocmulgee site, little is known. Most have been at least partially excavated, and some were virtually destroyed by road crews who used the dirt for road fill. Seven other earth lodges are now known at the site, none as elaborate as the one just described; only two contained seats, and none had an eagle platform opposite the entrance. One earth lodge was found at the Brown's Mount site a few miles from Ocmulgee.

Inside the structure, directly opposite the entrance, was a large, packed clay platform shaped to represent an eagle. It was 16 feet long, 14 feet wide, and 9–12 inches high. The head was toward the fire basin. ...The shoulders were slightly grooved as if to represent feathers, and the beak was shown by a shallow groove. The eye was a typical "forked eye" sunk 0.1 foot into the head. Just above the eye, a small hole 0.1 foot in diameter and 0.5 foot deep extended vertically into the head. At a distance of 4.5 feet from the wall was a row of three shallow rounded depressions 0.6 foot wide and 0.3 foot deep. The center one was 1.5 feet long, the other two were 1.3 feet long. On either side of the platform and extending around the wall to the entrance was a series of seats, twenty-three on the northerly and twenty-four on the southerly sides of the lodge. These seats were modeled on a clay bench raised 0.3–0.5 foot above the floor. Each seat was separated from the next by a low rounded curb 0.6 foot wide and 0.3 foot high. Each seat had, at the front, an oval depression similar to the three on the eagle platform....The bench was slightly higher near the platform and lowest near the door. At two places on the front edge of the bench and at one place near the wall were found small post holes 0.6 foot in diameter. (Fairbanks 1946: 95)

Pottery associated with these sites is unlike that of preceding or contemporary sites in the area. Much of it was tempered with crushed mussel shell, and it is more like the pottery of the Tennessee River valley of this period. Most of this pottery is plain and undecorated.

Few features that could be identified as house structures were uncovered in the excavations, but ditches were found that had enclosed much of the central part of the site, typical of Mississippian ceremonial centers. Traditionally, such ditches have been interpreted as defensive, but at Ocmulgee that conclusion has been questioned. The ditches vary from about ten to twenty-five feet wide and from three to nine feet deep. Excavating the ditches and ditch segments proved difficult, for archaeologists found it almost impossible to determine the ditch profile in cross section. Erosion had occurred, and farming activities in the nineteenth and twentieth centuries had further obliterated and confused the archaeological record. No remains of a palisade were discernible, although palisades are common at other Mississippian sites, particularly around the ceremonial area. Any remains of a palisade, such as postholes, could also have been removed from the archaeological record by erosion and farming. David Hally, an archaeologist at the University of Georgia, has explored the

Fig. 5.3. Long-necked jar from the Ocmulgee site (courtesy National Park Service)

A number of the traits practiced by the Ocmulgee people did, however, continue elsewhere in the area as subsequent waves of Mississippian influence inundated the Southeast. The two most distinctive
Mississippian traits—intensive agriculture and ceremonial mound-
building and accompanying religious beliefs—found wide acceptance
throughout the region. Mississippian ideas were incorporated into the
old Woodland ways, and the resultant hybrid cultures proved durable
and adaptive. Successful farming led to population growth, which led
to more elaborate social and ideological structures and a proliferation
of art forms. In Georgia, this trend reached a peak during the thir-
teenth and fourteenth centuries, the high point of the Etowah culture.
(O'Connor 1995: 118)

---

problem of interpreting these ditches and concluded that they probably
were defensive in nature (see Hally 1994: 91–93).

Archaeologists have identified several other Early Mississippian cultures. The Averett culture, in the Chattahoochee River valley near the Fall
Line, apparently represents another of the transitional manifestations
between Woodland and Mississippian. It is identified by incised, brushed,
or plain pottery, which is sometimes found with Etowah complicated-
stamped pottery, a type more common a hundred miles or so to the north.
No mounds have been found on sites belonging to this culture. Organic
remains from the Carmouche site (Muscogee County) demonstrate the
use of hickory nuts, acorns, persimmons, maize, deer, turtle, turkey, and
fish. Here again, indications are that agriculture played a minor role in the
economy. The Vining Phase, characterized by simple-stamped pottery, is
believed to represent a Woodland-Mississippian transitional culture in the
lower central Piedmont (Putnam County area).

The Etowah culture follows Woodstock in the upper Piedmont. It is
identified by line-block and ladder-based diamond complicated-stamped
designs on pottery, and sherds bearing these design elements have often
been found mixed with Woodstock pottery. Some archaeologists classify
the "early Etowah" pottery as Woodstock. The later Etowah Phase is
better understood, however, for the pottery is more distinguishable—
plain, polished, red-filmed, and, when complicated-stamped, often bearing a two-bar diamond motif.

Fig. 5.4. Etowah complicated-stamped pottery (courtesy Laboratory of Archaeology, Department of Anthropology, University of Georgia; photo by David Price)

In the Georgia Coastal Plain, the Early Mississippian is marked by the Standley Phase, a cultural manifestation along the lower Chattahoochee River. Standley Phase pottery is shell-tempered, a Mississippian characteristic, and was a component in the earliest levels at the Rood's Landing site in Stewart County. This site consists of eight mounds and several plaza areas; four of the mounds yielded evidence of structures on their summits. Farther downriver, the Wakulla Phase, typified by check-stamped pottery, is considered a transitional Woodland-Mississippian culture.

The Neisler Mound, a large site with a mound approximately twenty-five feet high, is situated on the Flint River in Taylor County. Archaeological investigations in the early twentieth century indicated that its earliest components belong to the Etowah Phase of the Mississippian. More recent work here and at the Hartley-Posey Mound, also on the Flint River in Taylor County, has demonstrated that the sites belong to the Late Etowah Phase of the Mississippian, dated to about A.D. 1150. Other Etowah Phase sites occur along the lower Flint River. Elsewhere in the Coastal Plain, Mississippian sites are not common.

Along the Georgia coast, the Early Mississippian is marked by the Savannah Phase, which is seen as having developed out of the Late Woodland Wilmington Phase. The Savannah Phase is characterized by the appearance of large settlements around temple mounds, with smaller settlements located in the surrounding region. In addition to cord-marked pottery, check-stamped, complicated-stamped, and burnished-plain pottery began to be manufactured.

Middle Mississippian (A.D. 1200–1350)

The Middle Mississippian was a time of increasing social complexity and population growth. More village sites appear, many with temple mounds, and burials in and around the mounds are often accompanied by distinctive artifacts. The temporal or regional expressions of Middle Mississippian culture are reflected in differences in pottery decoration, again widely used by archaeologists as a time indicator. In the northern half of Georgia, the Savannah culture dates to Middle Mississippian times and is identified by four pottery types: Savannah complicated-stamped, Savannah plain, Savannah check-stamped, and Etowah complicated-stamped.

One of the most thoroughly investigated sites of the Middle Mississippian is the Beaverdam Creek site, located on a small tributary of the upper Savannah River in Elbert County. Excavations conducted there during the 1970s and 1980s, before its inundation by the Russell Reservoir, focused on a mound that had been heavily damaged by pot hunters. Excavations into what remained of the mound revealed that the initial structure on the site might have been an earth lodge similar to those on the Macon Plateau and to those at other sites of this time period. Over the remains of this structure, a platform mound was constructed. Ultimately, four stages of mound construction could be discerned, and thirty-seven burials were encountered. One burial was obviously that of a high-status individual, for grave furnishings included an embossed, crescent-shaped copper head ornament, two embossed copper-covered wooden earspools, a seashell necklace, and a shell gorget. Excavations in the adjacent village area encountered an additional ten burials but no identifiable house structures.

One of the largest and most impressive sites of the Middle Mississippian in Georgia is the Etowah site just outside Cartersville (Bartow County). It has been the scene of archaeological investigations since the late 1800s, when John P. Rogan of the Bureau of American Ethnology carried out some exploratory excavations. Much more work was done by Warren K. Moorehead of the Phillips Academy in Andover, Massachusetts, in the 1920s. In the 1950s, A. R. Kelly and Lewis H. Larson excavated what remained of Mound C for the Georgia Historical Commission. Small-scale excavations took place in the 1970s and 1980s, mostly under the direction of Roy Dickens of Georgia State University. In 1994, Adam King excavated at Mounds A and B for the Georgia Department of Natural Resources. His excavations revealed some of the original stairway on Mound A. All the excavations have generated information (and raised more questions) about the Etowah site, one of the most important archaeological sites in the greater Southeast.

The Etowah site lies on the banks of the Etowah River and consists of three mounds. Three smaller mounds on the site have been obliterated. The ceremonial area covers about forty acres and was originally surrounded by a moat or ditch thirty feet wide and ten feet deep and overlooked by an impressive log stockade with bastions. The ceremonial area was thus bordered by the river on one side and protected by the stockade and moat on all other sides.

The largest mound at the site, Mound A, measures 380 by 330 feet at the base and is a little over 60 feet high. Archaeologists believe that the mound was originally about 75 feet high, but the summit was plowed and cultivated for many years by the family who owned the property before the state acquired it. This undoubtedly led to erosion and to the present uneven aspect of the summit. Mound A was first described in 1819 by Rev. Elias Cornelius, who was taken to the site by some Indian leaders: "Judging from the degree of its declivity, the perpendicular height cannot be less than seventy-five feet. . . . Its top is level, and at the time I visited it, was so completely covered with weeds, bushes, and trees of most luxuriant growth, that I could not examine it as well as I wished. Its diameter, I judged, must be one hundred and fifty feet" (quoted in Wauchope 1966: 251–52). Mound A has not been excavated, although limited excavations were conducted on the summit in the early 1970s to see if the remains of a structure could be uncovered. The results of this work remain unpublished, but apparently no structural remains were encountered. Other excavations just in front of the mound revealed a 3-foot-high square plaza of clay extending 330 feet on each side, undoubtedly the sacred plaza where important and colorful ceremonies took place.

The second-largest mound remaining at Etowah, Mound B, has not been fully excavated, but Kelly and Larson conducted limited excavations into one side, where they found evidence of "residential debris containing few ceremonial objects." The burials they uncovered here were not elaborate and were evidently from a later period (the Late Mississippian Lamar Phase). In other words, these burials belonged to a people who lived on the site after the height of cultural development during the Middle Mississippian, and who simply buried their dead in or around the monuments from earlier times. Saucer-shaped pits near the base of Mound B contained large quantities of "animal bone, ethnobo-

Fig. 5.5. Mound B at the Etowah site, Bartow County (courtesy Georgia Department of Natural Resources)

tanical materials, bone tools and shell and stone objects, as well as tons of broken pottery. Practically all of this appears to be the detritus of daily living" (Kelly and Larson 1956: 45). Thus, Mound B is believed to have served as the residence site of a political/religious leader during the Middle Mississippian.

Mound C at the Etowah site has received the most attention from archaeologists. Warren Moorehead dug here in the 1920s (his "excavation" methods make contemporary archaeologists shudder) and encountered richly furnished burials. He apparently believed that little was left to be discovered after his work was finished, for in his published report he states that the mound probably contained only a few remaining burials. Mound C was originally about 150 feet square at the base and about 18 feet high. By the time excavations began in the 1950s, much of the mound had been lost to previous excavations and to erosion caused by flooding. Prior to its acquisition by the state, this entire site, including the mounds, had been plowed and cultivated since the first white settlement in the area in the early 1800s. With no groundcover except rows of corn or other crops, the entire site was highly susceptible to erosion, particularly when the Etowah River flooded.

Fig. 5.6. Copper axes, some with portions of the handle intact, from the Etowah site (courtesy Georgia Department of Natural Resources and the Antonio J. Waring Jr. Archaeological Laboratory)

Fig. 5.7. Engraved shell gorget depicting a costumed dancer, from the Etowah site (courtesy Georgia Department of Natural Resources and the Antonio J. Waring Jr. Archaeological Laboratory)

Moorehead's investigations revealed richly furnished burials in Mound C, with copper, shell, and other artifacts identified as belonging to the "Southern Cult" ceremonial complex. In one place, his workers found a human effigy of stone placed in a carefully constructed grave lined with stone slabs. In his report, Moorehead draws some intriguing parallels between what he found in Mound C and practices of the Creek Indians known from early historic accounts ([1932] 1979:79). Included are descriptions of the temples atop some mounds and a discussion on mounds and their functions, the use of copper, the significance of the eagle, the arrangement of villages around a plaza, and various legends that seem to tie in with objects or art motifs found in Mound C.

The several periods of excavation revealed 350 burials; 210 of these were recovered by the Georgia Historical Commission excavations in the 1950s. These excavations, supervised by A. R. Kelly and Lewis Larson, revealed that Mound C had been constructed in five stages, each marked by the addition of a new layer of clay over the whole structure and probably by the construction of a new building on the summit. A log palisade encircled the base of the mound, and in later stages of mound construction numerous burials were placed just inside this palisade and around the mound's base. Because of the large number of burials associated with this mound, the remains of a building on the summit, and the encircling log wall, archaeologists believe that it was the site of a mortuary temple like those described in the early historic literature. In Kelly and Larson's excavations, the final burials around the base of Mound C were found to be the most elaborate, for they contained all the artifacts associated with the Southern Cult or Southeastern Ceremonial Complex. The ceramics found in these burials make it possible to assign them to the Wilbanks Phase of the Middle Mississippian.

Burials included adults as well as children, and presumably both men and women, although skeletal preservation was poor and gender determination was uncertain. Grave goods included ceremonial weapons and ornaments from costumes. In the latter category were copper-covered earspools and engraved shell gorgets; necklaces and pendants of shell; copper-covered wooden beads and beaded bands on the arms and legs; the remains of headdresses; hair ornaments; cut-outs of copper, sea-turtle shell, and mica; and copper-covered wooden rattles. One such rattle was carved in the shape of a human face. A poorly preserved copper headdress with horns was found in one tomb, the remains of a fanlike feather headdress with copper ornaments in another. The ceremonial weapons found

Fig. 5.8. Embossed copper badge representing eagle (?) claws, from the Etowah site (courtesy Georgia Department of Natural Resources and the Antonio J. Waring Jr. Archaeological Laboratory)

Fig. 5.9. Stone palette from the Etowah site (courtesy Georgia Department of Natural Resources and the Antonio J. Waring Jr. Archaeological Laboratory)

The burials are of two types—in simple rectangular pits and in more elaborate log tombs. The latter were constructed by erecting logs vertically in a wall trench around the edge of a pit. Other logs placed horizontally across the top formed a roof. Each burial was made parallel to the side of the mound. Only a few of the seventy-five burials found to date contained more than one individual. The preservation of the skeletal material is uniformly poor. The decayed roof timbers of the log tombs had collapsed, damaging not only the skeletons but the grave goods as well.

One of the most remarkable of the log tombs was Burial No. 38, on the north side of the mound. The pit was some ten feet square, with forty-two small posts set upright in a wall trench around the edge of the pit floor. The logs forming the roof had collapsed and were lying on the floor, covered by the clay overburden. Arranged on the floor were five skeletons, each accompanied by a copper celt with part of the wooden handle preserved. A polished stone disc with a scalloped edge (ten inches in diameter) lay near one skull. A lump of graphite and a lump of galena (lead ore) found under the disc showed that it must have served as a palette for the preparation of face or body paint. With each skull were the remains of an elaborate headdress formed of pieces of copper cut out and embossed. Copper-covered wooden beads set with seed pearls were also found, as well as a conch-shell gorget bearing an excised cross design, fragments of split cane matting, numerous shell beads and a large conch shell.

Three other scalloped palettes were found in other tombs, as well as three more shell gorgets, five copper axes, two copper-covered stone celts, or axes, and two copper headdresses.

In another log tomb we encountered what is perhaps our most important single find. Associated with the remains of three dismembered bodies were two large marble figures, one representing a man, the other a woman. Each stands two feet high and weighs close to one hundred pounds. The discovery of these figures occasioned perhaps the only instance in the history of Southeastern archaeology when a single artifact could not be removed from the excavation except by wheelbarrow! The woman is represented as kneeling, with hands on knees. She wears a skirt with a belt. She has a flat, disc-shaped headdress and a knapsack-like object on her back. The man, a larger figure, is seated cross-legged, with hands on knees. His curious headdress includes a coil or bunch (of hair?) on the back of the head. On both figures the ears are painted red, the eyes white with black pupils, and other details are greenish black, carbon black, red or white. Both figures are well carved and polished, with details carefully rendered. Their rather stiff and bulky appearance lacks the grace and fluid lines of the human figures represented on the embossed copper plates and gorgets from Etowah. (Kelly and Larson 1956; reprinted courtesy of *Archaeology*)

included long, chipped-flint blades, copper celts, spatulate stone celts, and monolithic axes (handle and blade fashioned from a single piece of stone). The archaeologists concluded that all were of a form or material that precluded their use as tools or weapons and that their purpose therefore was ceremonial.

Larson (1971) believes that the burials in and around Mound C represent those of a kin group that formed the powerful political, religious, and economic leadership at Etowah. Exotic grave goods (copper, seashell, mica, flint blades) are not found except in the burials of the elite. Limited excavations in the village area at the Etowah site revealed that the residents were buried without any grave goods except an occasional small utilitarian bowl. The presence of exotic, and especially nonlocal, items in the graves of the elite suggests that this group was in control of obtaining, consuming, and possibly trading this material to other societies in the region. Larson further speculates that the presence of these items at other

Fig. 5.10. (*left*) Male effigy from the Etowah site (courtesy Georgia Department of Natural Resources and the Antonio J. Waring Jr. Archaeological Laboratory)

Fig. 5.11. (*right*) Male effigy, side view (courtesy Georgia Department of Natural Resources and the Antonio J. Waring Jr. Archaeological Laboratory)

sites could well result from a regional system of exchange among the leaders of the societies involved.

There are numerous other sites in Georgia, particularly in the northern half of the state, that were part of the Southeastern Ceremonial Complex. Many contain one or more mounds, and burials have yielded paraphernalia similar to that found at Etowah. One of the earliest scientific investigations of a mound site was conducted at the Hollywood Mound group just south of Augusta. This site consisted of two temple mounds situated in a bend of the Savannah River. Henry L. Reynolds, of the Bureau of American Ethnology, who excavated the smaller mound at this site in the late 1800s, found that it had been constructed in three stages. The earliest mound level contained elaborate artifacts of the Southeastern Ceremonial Complex, including copper plates, effigy vessels, and pipes. In some instances, the copper salts had preserved fragments of cloth, basketry, and other perishable materials.

Fig. 5.12. (*left*) Female effigy from the Etowah site (courtesy Georgia Department of Natural Resources and the Antonio J. Waring Jr. Archaeological Laboratory)

Fig. 5.13. (*right*) Female effigy, side view (courtesy Georgia Department of Natural Resources and the Antonio J. Waring Jr. Archaeological Laboratory)

Fig. 5.14. Cloth fragment from the Etowah site (courtesy Georgia Department of Natural Resources and the Antonio J. Waring Jr. Archaeological Laboratory)

Other sites with mounds that date to this period in northern Georgia include Scull Shoals (Greene County), Shinholser (Baldwin County), Bell Field (Murray County), and Two Run Creek (Bartow County). Most sites in the north did not contain mounds but appear to be small villages or individual dwellings situated along creeks and small tributaries with patches of bottomland. Larger villages with mounds are almost always located on larger streams with extensive bottomlands, undoubtedly chosen as agricultural sites that could supply food for a much larger aggregation of people. (It is estimated that the population at the Etowah site and subsidiary sites scattered up and down the river might have reached 15,000.) Some of the smaller villages contained a single mound. Some Mississippian villages were palisaded, such as the one excavated at Ruckers Bottom (Elbert County), although this site contained no mound. This pattern of palisaded villages, witnessed by the first Europeans in the Southeast, is undoubtedly a testimonial to the ever-present danger of raids, even in late prehistoric times.

In the Georgia Coastal Plain, mature Mississippian sites are less in evidence. Joseph R. Caldwell investigated the Rood's Landing site in Stewart County, a multiple-mound site, in the 1950s. His excavations revealed the remains of three structures on the top of Mound A constructed of wattle and daub (clay mixed with Spanish moss plastered over a latticework of cane). One structure at this site was teardrop shaped, another was rectangular, and the third was square. Because of its distinctive characteristics, the Rood's Landing site gave rise to the concept of the Rood Phase of the Mississippian in this part of Georgia. Much more information on the Rood Phase was obtained from the Cemochechobee site.

On the banks of the Chattahoochee River in Clay County, the Cemochechobee site consisted of a village area and three mounds, two of which were eroding into the river. Investigations into these two mounds by the Columbus Museum began in the late 1970s. Mound A was found to be a burial mound, Mound B a platform mound composed of ten distinctive stages of construction. Excavations here revealed the remains of a ceremonial compound, a mortuary house, and some burials with Southeastern Ceremonial Complex items, including the remains of a headdress with copper ornaments, effigy pots, and celts.

In nearby Stewart County, the Columbus Museum also excavated the Singer-Moye site, another multiple-mound site, where archaeologists found the remains of a type of earth lodge. It consisted of a large square structure of wattle and daub, around which earth was piled. After the roof had collapsed, the whole interior was filled with earth, forming a dome-shaped mound that apparently was never used again.

Elsewhere in the Coastal Plain, Middle Mississippian sites are apparently few. Some Etowah Phase sites exist on the lower Flint River, one containing a large mound. In the Okefenokee Swamp, archaeological work has revealed several mounds, but most of these are associated with the Weeden Island culture and are thus somewhat earlier than the Middle Mississippian. Only a few sites in the Okefenokee can be attributed to the Middle or Late Mississippian.

Along the Georgia coast, the Savannah Phase follows the Wilmington Phase of the Woodland. Some archaeologists argue for a transitional St. Catherines Phase, but others see little justification for this assumption. The Savannah Phase persists through Middle Mississippian times, at the end of which it is replaced by the Late Mississippian Irene Phase. The Late Savannah Phase saw a great increase in population. It is especially evident at sites in McIntosh and Glynn Counties, where there are numerous sites of this period, some containing mounds.

Late Mississippian (A.D. 1350–1550)

It is with the Late Mississippian that things begin to look more familiar to us, for there appears to be considerable carryover to the tribes who

Fig. 5.15. Spiral mound at the Lamar site, Bibb County (courtesy National Park Service)

lived in Georgia in the Early Historic Period. During the last century or so before European contact, peoples were following essentially the same way of life as that witnessed and at least partially recorded by the first explorers and traders. The archaeological record is thus a little easier to interpret.

In the Late Mississippian of the Georgia Piedmont, Blue Ridge Mountains, and Ridge and Valley province, a single cultural tradition is recognized—the Lamar. Defined primarily on the basis of pottery, it is characterized by designs referred to as Lamar complicated-stamped, Lamar incised, and Lamar plain. While incised decorations are sometimes finely executed, at other times they are not. There are several regional variants, but much of the pottery is rather rough and sloppily decorated when compared to earlier ceramic types.

The Lamar culture takes its name from the Lamar site, located about three miles from the Macon Plateau or Ocmulgee site. It is on a low hill surrounded by swamp, and so it is believed to have been an island in the swamp during its prehistoric occupation. Excavations here in the 1930s revealed thirty burials, along with the remains of rectangular houses. Two mounds dominate the site. The larger is the typical rectangular temple mound, but the smaller mound is conical and flat topped, with a spiral

Fig. 5.16. Lamar complicated-stamped pottery (from a private collection; photo by David Price)

Fig. 5.17. Lamar bold-incised pottery (courtesy Piedmont College; photo by David Price)

ramp winding to the summit. The earliest occupation level contained Swift Creek pottery, which was followed by Macon Plateau ceramics. The final occupation was marked by the presence of pottery decorated in styles now identified as Lamar and consisting of complicated-stamped and incised designs.

The village area at the Lamar site was completely surrounded by a log palisade 3,560 feet long, enclosing a little more than twenty-one acres. Postholes were six to twelve inches in diameter and were set about one foot apart. There was some evidence that the swamp paralleling the pali-

Fig. 5.18. Mississippian pipes (courtesy Georgia Department of Natural Resources)

sade had been artificially deepened in some places, giving it a moatlike aspect and presumably enhancing the defenses of the island. The archaeologists involved in excavating this site concluded that it was a religious-political center and village that probably served as a refuge for people in outlying settlements and farmsteads when a raid or attack was imminent.

Evidence indicates that Lamar peoples were heavily dependent upon agriculture, but they continued to hunt, fish, and gather wild plant foods on a rather intensive basis. Deer was the main source of meat, with turkey, fish, and other species being of lesser importance. Houses were square and constructed of wattle and daub.

The Lamar sites that contain platform mounds have received the most attention from the archaeologists. Excavations in these Lamar mounds indicate a decline in the importance of the Southeastern Ceremonial Complex. Mound burials are not as richly furnished as those of earlier times, but some art motifs and artifacts of this ceremonial system continued in use. The Little Egypt site in northwest Georgia (Murray County), which belongs to the Lamar culture of the Late Mississippian, consisted of three mounds and a village area. Pottery from this site included the Dallas type derived from east Tennessee, in addition to the common Lamar types seen

About four feet east of this grave, but at a depth of 17 ft. 5 in. from the summit of the mound to the bottom of the grave, and 14 ft. 9 in. beneath the slope ... was another stone-box grave (Burial 39), measuring only 4 ft. 7 in. by 3 ft. 10 in., by 2 ft. 5 in. wide. In some respects this interment was the most interesting of the many uncovered at Nacoochee, by reason of the finding, among other objects, of an earthenware effigy vessel of painted ware, the only specimen of painted pottery, with the exception of a small sherd recovered from the same section of the mound and at approximately the same depth, found during the entire exploration. The body had been laid on its right side, with the head directed eastwardly, on a layer of bark placed on the earthen floor. The bones of the trunk had almost disappeared through decay, but were sufficiently traceable to indicate that the body had been bowed greatly outward, while the upper leg-bones, which were in somewhat better condition, were flexed strongly upward and the lower leg-bones lay against the pelvis. This distortion was evidently necessary because of the small size of the grave. The skull, which was of the consistency of cornmeal owing to decay and the ravages of insects, lay in the upper left-hand or northwest corner of the cist. (Heye, Hodge, and Pepper 1918: 19–20)

elsewhere in Georgia. In the same region, the King site (Floyd County) belonged to the Lamar culture but had no mound; the village was encircled by a ditch and palisade. Archaeologists estimate that the village represented at the King site consisted of up to fifty houses arranged around a large central plaza.

In the northeast Georgia mountains, the Nacoochee site in White County was the scene of archaeological investigations early in the twentieth century. Seventy-five burials were excavated in this Late Mississippian mound. Several were in graves lined with slabs of stone, and some contained dog-effigy pots like those encountered elsewhere in Late Mississippian burial contexts.

In the middle Chattahoochee River valley of the Coastal Plain, the Bull Creek Phase is recognized as a Late Mississippian cultural expression. Dating to about A.D. 1400–1475, the phase takes its name from the Bull

Creek site near Columbus (Muscogee County). Although heavily damaged by railroad construction and other commercial operations, enough of the site remained to attract the attention of archaeologists at intervals through much of the twentieth century. The site was that of a village and apparently did not contain a mound. However, burials encountered in the excavations sometimes contained dog-effigy ceramic vessels similar to those found elsewhere in burials of the elite in or near mounds. The most common pottery found on this site is Lamar, but Fort Walton types are present, indicating the position of the Bull Creek site between cultural traditions emanating from north and south of the Fall Line. Elsewhere in the Coastal Plain, Lamar sites are known along the Ocmulgee River, including the Lamar-type site near Macon.

The Late Mississippian on the Georgia coast is represented by the Irene Phase, named for the Irene Mound site on the Savannah River near the city of Savannah. The scene of excavations from 1937 to 1940, this site is bounded on three sides by the river and Pipemakers Creek and bordered by an old streambed to the south; it was virtually an island, particularly during seasonal floods and at high tide. The site covered some six acres and consisted of two mounds and the remains of other structures. Before it was excavated, the large mound was nearly circular, round topped, 15½ feet high and 160 feet in diameter. The smaller mound, 2½ feet high and 55 feet in diameter, proved to be a burial site, and 106 interments were found here. Excavation revealed that the large mound had been constructed in eight stages. Remains of structures and palisades were common in this mound.

Near the large mound, archaeologists found the remains of a mortuary structure that dated to a very late occupation of the Irene site, contemporaneous with or later than the final layer of the mound. The building had been burned, perhaps intentionally, and a sand fill had been used to cover the ruins, which preserved skeletal material very well. Early Europeans who visited among the southeastern Indians described mortuary structures where the skeletal remains of ancestors were kept. It was the practice among some groups to ceremonially burn the building when it was full, then construct a new building on the same site.

Pottery at the Irene site belonged primarily to the Savannah and Irene ceramic complexes. Regarding Irene pottery, the authors of the report wrote, "The Irene period is historic or nearly so and roughly coincides with the occupation of the 'Lamar-like' sites of central Georgia" (Caldwell and McCann 1941: 40).

The mortuary was built in a shallow excavation from ten to sixteen inches deep. This penetrated several inches of older refuse deposits and cut into virgin sand. Wall posts five to seven inches thick were set at the edges of the sunken floor and spaced about eight inches apart, forming a square with rounded corners. Each side of the building was approximately twenty-four feet long. In several places the wall was represented by a single row of posts, in others by double or triple rows. Whether the multiple rows of posts represented corrections in the initial placement or later repairs is not known. Wall trenches were not used in the construction of the wall. The depth of the posts below the floor of the structure ranged from nineteen to twenty-three inches. A fallen beam, found in the northeast corner, indicated that the wall posts projected at least five feet, six inches above the floor. In four cases actual unrotted, unburned sections of posts were found in the postholes. They were of yellow pine and satisfactory for dendrochronological analysis.

Standing wall plaster was found intact to a height of fourteen inches in several places along the interior of the wall. It was fired to a brick red or bright orange. The thickness of the interior plastering was about one and one-half inches. Impressions of reeds and wall posts in the fired plastering indicated a typical wattle and daub structure. Bundles of reeds or possibly wild grape vines had been interlaced at relatively short intervals between the uprights. The plastering itself consisted of clay of a sort which is readily available at the site. This clay, thoroughly kneaded, was heavily tempered with a vegetal binder, probably Spanish moss. It was then applied to the interior surface of the wall probably to the eaves, where it may have terminated at a longitudinal log or stringer to which the lower ends of the roof poles were bound. If the outside of the wall was covered at all, the covering probably consisted of a perishable material such as cane or palmetto matting. (Caldwell and McCann 1941:25)

Conclusion

The Mississippian time period witnessed a drastic change in the cultures of tribes in Georgia and the Southeast, who took up the agricultural way of life. Along with agriculture came a ceremonial system apparently at-tuned to the crop cycle, in which the sun was revered if not worshipped. Some of our conclusions about Mississippian ceremonialism are based on the writings of Spanish explorers, English traders, and other early visitors among the southeastern tribes who saw Mississippian culture flourishing. The situation would shortly change, for the European entrance would cut short the cultural florescence and finally result in the expulsion of most of the surviving tribes from the Southeast.

From its earliest expression at sites such as Ocmulgee and Woodstock, Mississippian culture was characterized by permanent settlements forti-fied by log palisades and ditches. Earth mounds were constructed at many sites to serve as temple platforms, burial places for the leaders of the soci-ety, and sometimes as platforms for the home of the leader of the group. People who live by farming must remain in the same location for much of the year. Successful agriculture yields a food surplus, and one result of residential stability and plenty of food is a population increase. This is certainly reflected in the archaeological record in Georgia, as Mississip-

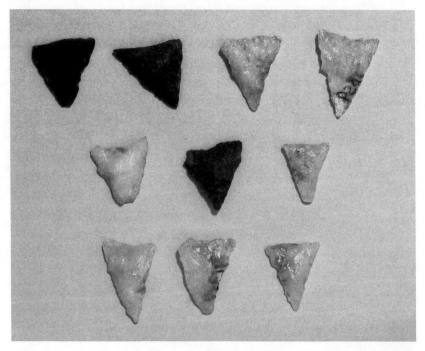

Fig. 5.19. Triangular projectile points of the Mississippian (from a private collec-tion; photo by David Price)

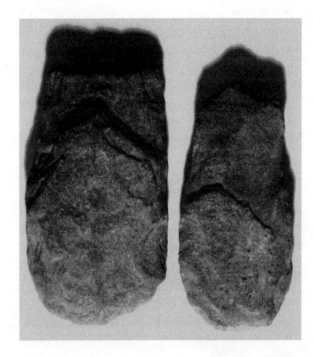

Fig. 5.20. Stone hoes (from a private collection; photo by David Price)

pian sites proliferated across the landscape. A typical pattern late in this period was a large riverside ceremonial center that served as the capital town, with attached towns, settlements, and farmsteads spread out for miles along the river and its tributaries. Most Mississippian settlements were situated in the river bottoms, where the best agricultural land was to be found. Upland forests were used as sources for firewood and building materials and for hunting. Although corn (maize), beans, squash, and a few other crops furnished most of the food, hunting, fishing, and gathering continued to be important for feeding the population. Acorns, for instance, remained a key element in the diet, following a pattern established at least by Early Archaic times.

Large towns with ceremonial centers, subsidiary smaller towns and villages, and richly furnished burials in or near the mounds suggest a level of society more complex than any seen up to this time in the Southeast. Archaeologists believe that it reflects the rise of a type of political-social organization called a chiefdom, which is characterized by a social ranking system and a chief with considerable power. Other characteristics include centralized control of resources and labor and the construction of public monuments and features such as mounds, palisades, moats, and ditches.

In Georgia, sites such as Etowah and Shinholser are considered to represent the capital towns of chiefdoms. Records left by members of the de Soto expedition lend further insight into Late Mississippian societies, and their descriptions are further evidence of the existence of chiefdoms as defined by anthropologists.

Suggestions for Further Reading

Caldwell, Joseph, and Catherine McCann. 1941. *Irene Mound Site, Chatham County, Georgia,* Athens: University of Georgia Press.

Cobb, Charles R., and Patrick H. Garrow. 1996. "Woodstock Culture and the Question of Mississippian Emergence." *American Antiquity* 61, 1: 21–37.

Kelly, A. R., and Lewis H. Larson, Jr. 1956. "Explorations at Etowah Indian Mounds near Cartersville, Georgia, Seasons 1954, 1955, 1956." *Archaeology* 10: 39–48.

Waring, Antonio J., Jr. 1968. *The Waring Papers: The Southern Cult and Other Archaeological Essays,* ed. Stephen Williams. Athens: University of Georgia Press.

White, Max E. 1988. *Georgia's Indian Heritage: The Prehistoric Peoples and Historic Tribes of Georgia.* Roswell, Ga.: Wolfe.

6

Contact and Early History

Smooth gray clouds, driven by a cool and brisk easterly wind, covered the sky. The newly foliaged trees rocked in the gusts, and the bright green leaves displayed their lighter undersides. A feeling of uneasiness pervaded the scene, particularly in the Indian village. The old wise men had related dreams they had had in recent weeks, all of which seemed to be warnings, and these came to mind when the people first heard rumors of strange men and even stranger beasts entering their country. Word passed from village to village, from tribe to tribe, containing stories of unbelievable cruelty on the part of these new people.

In this village, most of the women and children had fled into the surrounding forest and swamps to hide. People were unsure what to do, for they did not know why these strange beings had come to them, or what course of action to take. Most of the warriors had remained in the village to see what would happen, and as they waited expectantly, talking in low voices, dogs began to bark on the outskirts of the settlement. The strangers had arrived. One warrior peered from behind a house near the square ground and saw the vanguard enter the village where the trail from the southwest opened into the clearing.

First contact between the Indian tribes of Georgia and Europeans was not a pleasant experience. The European presence began when the expedition of Lucas Vázquez de Ayllón briefly visited the coast in 1526. Of much greater importance, however, was the expedition of Hernando de Soto that traversed the state in the summer of 1540. De Soto, exceedingly cruel and heartless, promoted only fear and hatred in the native population.

The most devastating result of his expedition was what amounted to germ warfare, although it was unintentional. Members of the de Soto expedition apparently spread smallpox and other Old World diseases, and within a few years the southeastern tribes had been decimated by the tens of thousands. Isolated from the Old World for many thousands of years, they had no resistance to the diseases brought by the Europeans. They also had no treatments. Like Europeans at the time of the Black Death of the Middle Ages, they had no idea what was causing their sickness, how it spread, or how it could be treated. We can only imagine the anguish of the tribes as thousands sickened and died. With no form of writing, the people passed their collective knowledge from generation to generation by word of mouth. As death claimed old and young alike, with the elderly went much of the accumulated knowledge of the people. It is small wonder that in later years, local Indians sometimes expressed ignorance of the builders of the ancient temple mounds. The Indians encountered by the English in the eighteenth century were merely the survivors.

De Soto entered Georgia in the spring of 1540, as the expedition of about 600 people moved out of Florida. Not all were soldiers, and as the expedition progressed Indians were captured and enslaved to serve as porters and guides. Attempts have been made in recent years to identify the route of this expedition. Caution must be exercised in any such endeavor, for one must take into account changes in place-names and landscape, and distances mentioned in the records of this expedition remain uncertain at best. Charles Hudson of the University of Georgia has made the best attempt at reconstructing de Soto's route. He tried to match archaeological sites with places visited by the de Soto expedition, not only in Georgia but in all the other states as well.

It is fairly certain that de Soto spent the winter of 1539–40 at an Indian village at what is now Tallahassee, Florida. In the spring, he marched northward and after several days entered an area controlled by the chiefdom of Capachequi. Centered on the Chickasawhatchee Swamp, it was a

---

On Monday, the twenty-ninth of March, they left from there for Ichisi, and it rained so much, and a small river swelled in such a manner, that if they had not made much haste to cross, all of the army would have been endangered. This day Indian men and women came forth to receive them. The women came clothed in white, and they made a fine appearance, and they gave to the Christians tortillas of corn and some bundles of spring onions exactly like those of Castile, as fat as the tip of the thumb and more. And that was a food which helped them much from then on; and they ate them with tortillas, roasted and stewed and raw, and it was a great aid to them because they are very good. The white clothing in which those Indian women came clothed are some blankets of both coarse and fine linen. They make the thread of them from the bark of the mulberry trees; not from the outside but rather from the middle; and they know how to process and spin and prepare it so well and weave it, that they make very pretty blankets. And they put one on from the waist down, and another tied by one side and the top placed upon the shoulders, like those Bohemians or Egyptians who are in the habit of sometimes wandering through Spain. The thread is such that he who found himself there certified to me that he saw the women spin it from that bark of mulberry trees and make it as good as the most precious thread from Portugal that the women in Spain procure in order to sew, and some more thin and even, and stronger. The mulberry trees are exactly like those of Spain, and as large and larger; but the leaf is softer and better for silk, and the mulberries better for eating and even larger than those from Spain, and the Spaniards also made good use of them many times, in order to sustain themselves. They arrived that day at a town of a cacique subject to Ichisi, a pretty town and with plenty of food, and he [the cacique] gave them willingly of what he had, and they rested there on Tuesday, and then on Wednesday, the last day of March, the Governor and his army departed, and they arrived at the Great River, where they had many canoes in which they crossed very well and arrived at the town of the lord, who was one-eyed, and he gave them very good food and fifteen Indians to carry the burdens. And as he was the first who came in peace, they did not wish to be tiresome. They were there Thursday, the first of April, and they placed a cross on the mound [cerro] of the town and informed them through the interpreter of the sanctity of the cross, and they received it and appeared to adore it with much devotion. (Rangel, quoted in Clayton, Knight, and Moore 1993: 271–72; reprinted courtesy of the University of Alabama Press)

fairly small chiefdom. As was to be a pattern for much of the journey, the Spaniards found Indian towns deserted and helped themselves to the food left behind. The Indians were wisely hiding in the forests or swamps until the expedition left. Pushing on northward, de Soto encountered the chiefdoms of Toa, Ichisi, Ocute, and Cofaqui. Hudson identifies Ichisi as the Lamar site near Macon and Ocute and Cofaqui as possibly the Shoulderbone and Dyar Mound sites, respectively.

In mid-April 1540, the de Soto expedition crossed what was probably the Savannah River, and during the next three months it traversed portions of South Carolina, North Carolina, and eastern Tennessee before reentering Georgia in mid-July. Passing from east Tennessee into northwest Georgia, de Soto came to the capital town of the Coosa chiefdom, almost certainly the major archaeological site near Carter's Dam in Murray County. His entrance into the town of Coosa is described in an account of the expedition by a "Gentleman of Elvas": "He reached Coça on Friday, July 16. The cacique came out to welcome him two crossbow flights from the town in a carrying chair borne on the shoulders of his principal men, seated on a cushion, and covered with a robe of marten skins of the form and size of a woman's shawl. He wore a crown of feathers on his head; and around him were many Indians playing and singing" (quoted in Clayton, Knight, and Moore 1993: 92).

After spending just over a month at Coosa, the de Soto expedition traveled southward, taking the chief of Coosa and other important personages along as hostages. On August 21, 1540, they arrived at the town of Itaba, identified as the Etowah site near Cartersville. This major center had declined from the height of its power and dominance, and at the time of the Spanish visit the Etowah site was a small village subject to Coosa. After waiting for floodwaters to recede, the expedition crossed the river and continued, stopping at two other towns, one of which might have been the King site near Rome. Soon thereafter, de Soto and his entourage entered what is now Alabama.

The chroniclers of de Soto's expedition did not record much detail in describing the country and its inhabitants. Anthropologists can draw conclusions from their writing, but no complete and satisfactory descriptions of Indian life exist. We do know that in 1540, chiefdoms were found wherever the Spanish went in Georgia. Each controlled a certain territory and exacted tribute from all the towns within that territory. Apparently, warfare existed between chiefdoms, which were sometimes separated by a no-man's-land where there were no settlements. Despite this belligerency, contact and trade existed, and Georgia was criss-crossed by well-used Indian trails.

De Soto's was only the first of several Spanish expeditions into Georgia. In 1597, Fray Pedro de Chozas, a missionary, led a small expedition from the Georgia coast to the town of Ocute, nine days' march inland. Chozas thought it prudent to heed the warning of Indians there to turn back, and he returned to the mission of San Pedro on what is now Cumberland Island. In July 1602, another expedition was sent to the Indian towns visited by Chozas, this one led by Juan de Lara, who explored northward from the town of Olatama, believed by some to have been on the Oconee River near the Fall Line. In 1604, Governor Ybarra left St. Augustine to visit the Guale province on the Georgia coast. He apparently wanted to lead another expedition into the interior, but there were delays in getting soldiers for his proposed journey, and it was never carried out.

With the establishment of the Jamestown settlement in Virginia in 1607, Spanish officials became concerned about the English presence on the east coast. Beginning in 1624, no fewer than five military expeditions were sent inland to investigate rumors of horsemen. None was found. In 1627, the final Spanish military expedition to explore the interior of the Southeast embarked, led by Pedro de Torres. This group apparently followed the route of the previous expeditions, going inland and northward from the Georgia coast. It went on, however, to visit the town of Cofitachequi, believed to have been well in the interior of what is now South Carolina. These expeditions all probably had a dual purpose. First, the Spanish wanted to explore the interior, and they especially wanted to investigate persistent rumors of gold and other riches in the mountains. Second, by exploring, claiming, and ultimately settling the land, the Spaniards hoped to solidify their claim to North America. This could be augmented by converting the Indians to Catholicism, and missions were established among the tribes of northern Florida and along the coast north of St. Augustine.

Although the historic record exists to verify these expeditions, there is little archaeological evidence of the Spanish presence in Georgia. Few Spanish artifacts have been recovered in archaeological excavations in Georgia's interior. In Murray County at the presumed site of Coosa, two silver crosses were found in a mound in 1832, according to the *Smithsonian Annual Report* for 1881 (see Wauchope 1966: 216–17). Originally believed to date from the Spanish period, these crosses are now considered to belong to the Cherokee occupation of the site, which occurred quite a bit later. Amateur archaeologists excavating an Indian burial in 1982 discovered a Spanish sword at the King site near Rome (Floyd County). The style of its hilt dated it to the de Soto era, and further study showed that the person with whom the sword was buried had been killed by a blow to the head by a sharp metal object, perhaps this very sword (see Little 1985). Archaeologists have found a few other European artifacts, noted in the literature as possibly Spanish, almost all in a few sites in northwest Georgia (see M. Smith 1992).

There is other indirect evidence of Spanish activity in northern Georgia and adjacent parts of North Carolina. In his historic work on the Cherokee, James Mooney wrote: "Long before the end of the sixteenth century, however, the existence of mines of gold and other metals in the Cherokee country was a matter of common knowledge among the Spaniards at St. Augustine and Santa Elena, and more than one expedition had been fitted out to explore the interior. Numerous traces of ancient mining operations, evidently of European origin, show that these discoveries were followed up, although the policy of Spain concealed the fact from the outside world" (1900: 29). In the early 1800s, a flood in Nacoochee Valley (White County) revealed that in the creek bank were logs that had been hewn and notched with a metal ax. It was concluded that the remains of these structures represented the Spanish presence.

The founding of St. Augustine in 1565 brought more sustained contact between the Spanish and the Indian tribes. Along with efforts to establish settlements, the Spanish began missionary work among the tribes, and in 1568 two Jesuits were stationed along the Georgia coast in Guale territory. Spanish records indicate the existence of forty or more villages in the Guale chiefdom. Although Swanton ([1922] 1998: 84) reported extensively on the Guale Indians, concluding that they were linguistically related to the Creek Indians and lived in a type of confederacy with a head chief, more recent scholarship concludes that the linguistic affiliation of the Guale remains unknown (Sturtevant 1996). The Jesuit missionaries had little success among the Guale and left in 1570. They were followed, however, by Franciscan missionaries, who by 1575 had baptized the chief of the Guale and his wife. The mission on the island of Guale (St. Catherines Island) came to be known as Santa Catalina de Guale; from 1595 the mission and settlement formed the primary northern outpost of the Spanish on the east coast.

All was not serene, however. As is often the case, the missionaries did not restrict their teaching to the religious realm but interfered in other areas of culture, fostering resentment among the Indians. When the Spanish executed several tribesmen near Guale in 1576, a rebellion broke out in which many Spaniards were killed. Hostilities extended all along the coast and included the settlement of Santa Elena, on what is now Parris Island, South Carolina. Despite some further attempts, missionaries did not return to the Guale coast until 1595, and most of them were killed when hostilities again broke out in 1597.

In 1605, Franciscan missionaries returned to their work among the Guale people and found the Indians more receptive. For the next several years, the trend was for mainland towns to be abandoned as the people moved onto the barrier islands, a move urged by the missionaries and made more expedient by further epidemics and, late in the century, by increasing attacks from enemy tribes sent against the mission settlements by the English. Attacks by the English and their Indian allies eventually led to the abandonment of the Guale coast by the Spanish and the remnants of the Guale Indians. Some of the Guale people, probably from the northern Georgia coast, sought refuge among the English. Others accompanied the Spaniards and moved to the outskirts of St. Augustine.

Archaeologists have searched for some time for the site of the mission of Santa Catalina de Guale. A University of Georgia expedition to St. Catherines Island in 1969 had as its purpose an archaeological reconnaissance survey, and limited investigations were undertaken at the Spanish site on Wamassee Creek, where it was believed the mission was located. While numerous Spanish and Indian artifacts were recovered, the mission site itself was not found. It remained for a team from the American Museum of Natural History led by David Hurst Thomas to find the site of the mission chapel a few years later. Extensive excavations revealed not only the church but also the friar's residence, the kitchen, and some Indian dwellings. Also excavated was the cemetery attached to the mission, and after analysis was completed, the remains were reburied in a ceremony presided over by the bishop of the Savannah Diocese before a congregation that included three Franciscan friars, representatives of the diocese, and others (see Thomas and Pendleton 1987). It is good that this important site is now known and has taken its deserved place in the annals of Georgia's early history.

The Spanish also established numerous missions among the Timucua Indians, a group occupying much of northern Florida and southeastern Georgia. Organized into numerous small chiefdoms, the Timucua became the object of intense missionary activity and missions were established throughout their territory, including southeastern Georgia. The subsequent history of the Timucua parallels to a great extent the history of the Guale. Eventually converted to Christianity and caught up in Spanish colonial interactions, the southeastern Georgia Timucua saw the erosion of their way of life and of their autonomy. Rebellion led to defeat at the hands of the Spaniards. The missions became the object of attacks and slave raids by Indian allies of the English, which led to Timucuan resettlement to missions in northern Florida. A series of devastating raids beginning in 1702 ended with the survivors moving to refugee villages around St. Augustine, where their numbers continued to decline. By 1726, a Spanish census listed 157 Timucua Indians, and in 1763, when the Spanish relinquished Florida to the English, only one Timucua is listed among the native peoples who accompanied the Spanish to Cuba (see Milanich 2000).

If the Spanish were interested primarily in extracting wealth in the form of gold and other minerals, the English were interested in extracting riches through trade with the Indian tribes. And they wanted land. With the establishment of Charles Town (Charleston, South Carolina) in 1670, the tribes of the interior Southeast were caught up in trade with the English to a greater extent than had been the case. The English traders were eager to trade for deerskins, and the Indians greatly desired the traders' iron skillets, pots and pans, and axes and knives, as well as their brightly colored cloth and beads. Another item offered by the traders was also greatly desired by some but came to cause serious problems—rum. The warriors liked its effect, but a social problem quickly developed as drunken warriors were easily cheated out of their deerskins by unscrupulous traders. Families were affected, as the desire for rum led men to neglect their responsibilities. The problems became so acute that chiefs sometimes petitioned the colonial authorities to stop the flow of rum to the tribes, but to no avail.

The other trade items had less noticeable but also serious consequences. As the tribes adopted European technology, they became dependent on the whites for these goods. As they came to use iron tools and other items, obviously more efficient than stone or bone tools or clay pots, the native people began to lose their self-sufficiency. Knowledge of how to make stone tools, clay pots, and other traditional items rapidly disappeared as the older generations died; the tribes became almost wholly dependent on trade goods for survival. This situation was exploited by the various colonial authorities, who gained concessions or promises of support from the Indians by merely threatening to cut off trade.

Tragically, the demand for labor by the English in Virginia led some groups to begin raiding enemy tribes for the primary purpose of obtaining captives, who would then be sold to the English as slaves. In Georgia, a group that gained notoriety for conducting slave raids is generally referred to as the Westo Indians, but scholars now believe that they were the same people as the Rickahockans, Rechaheckrians, and Chichimecos mentioned in the early historic literature. Now believed to have been a remnant Iroquoian group from the northeast, they were living in the Savannah Valley in the 1670s (see Bowne 2000). Armed by the English, they raided nearby tribes, especially those affiliated with Spanish missions. Possession of guns gave them an advantage over tribal groups without this technology. Widely known as aggressive slave raiders, their impact was drastic but short lived. By 1682, they were severely decimated, and soon thereafter they disappear from the historic record.

English traders were doing business with the Cherokees along the headwaters of the Savannah River by 1700, and by 1716 a trader lived at the Cherokee town of Tugalo on the Tugalo River (Stephens County). Along the coast, friction between the tribes and the English erupted in the

Fig. 6.1. Gen. James Oglethorpe meeting with Georgia Indians, from an old engraving (courtesy of Hargrett Rare Book and Manuscript Library/University of Georgia Libraries)

Yamassee War in 1715, which saw the Yamassee decisively defeated. They subsequently sought refuge in Florida. Other tribal groups who had plotted with the Yamassee moved their settlements to distance themselves from the English. Many of the groups known collectively as Creeks lived along the Ocmulgee River and its tributaries but now moved to the Chattahoochee River. Stability returned to the area with the peace agreement with the Creeks in 1717.

The native tribes remaining in Georgia inevitably became embroiled in the intrigues and wars of the European powers who competed for dominance in North America. With the founding of the Georgia colony and the establishment of Savannah in 1733, the English presence was much more imposing than that of the Spanish to the south or of the French to the west. In February of that year, General Oglethorpe landed at the site where Savannah would be built, and he almost immediately met Tomochichi, a chief of the Yamacraw Indians, whose village was nearby. The Yamacraw were apparently connected to the Creek Confederacy. Swanton believed in the 1920s that they might represent a surviving band of Yamassee (see Swanton [1922] 1998: 108–9), but more recent work suggests that they originated in some Creek towns. Tomochichi and his band had only recently moved to this vicinity, but he claimed the area as the land of his ancestors. Oglethorpe and Tomochichi apparently were friends from the start, and this connection facilitated relations between the infant colony and the Creeks. When Oglethorpe returned to England in 1734, he took Tomochichi with him.

The story of this visit bears a closer look, for it was important for both its impression on the Indians and its impact on the English. The party that left Savannah in March 1734 consisted of Tomochichi, his wife, his nephew, and a few warriors. Arriving in England in mid-June, the Indians were a sensation as they were shown about London. Dressed in their native attire, they were received by the Trustees of the Georgia Colony, King George II and Queen Caroline, and by the Archbishop of Canterbury. The visit created great excitement about the Georgia colony and resulted in a much larger financial grant from Parliament to increase defenses on the frontier, especially the southern border where the Spanish threat was greatest.

A high point of this visit must have been the audience with the king and queen at Kensington Palace. Tooanahowie, Tomochichi's nephew, recited the Lord's Prayer in English, after which the queen hugged him and the

Fig. 6.2. Georgia Indians meeting with the trustees of the Georgia colony, London, 1734 (courtesy Winterthur Museum)

Duke of Cumberland presented him with a gold watch. Later, Tomochichi spoke at Eton College, where he received a warm welcome. The visit came to a close when Tomochichi became homesick.

Tomochichi died October 5, 1739, and was buried in Savannah. Upon orders from General Oglethorpe, a state funeral was held and burial was in Persival Square with full military honors. The site is marked by a large stone on which a plaque bears this inscription: "In memory of Tomo-chi-chi the Mico of the Yamacraws, the companion of Oglethorpe and the friend and ally of the Colony of Georgia." Sadly, the Yamacraw band declined in numbers, and the remnants probably united with their Creek kin.

The years prior to the Revolutionary War saw more land cessions by the tribes of Georgia. With the coastal tribes extinct or reduced to refugee bands, the tribes of the interior grew increasingly alarmed at the ceaseless

May 26th 1772.

I went this Morning to the Pallachocola Square to black Drink where most of the head[s] of the Town were present. I informed them that I was going off this Day for Augusta, and desired that if they had any talks to send to Captain Stuart, that they would now acquaint me with them. They said that I had been in their Town but a Short time but had seen Nothing aMiss in their behaviour to me, they were but a poor people and had but very little to Intertain me with as they Could wish, but any thing which they had to spare I was wellcome to, and Likewise to Stay in their Town as long as I pleased. They desired me to acquaint Captain Stuart that they had used me well and desired that the Trade might not be stoped. They were now planting their Corn and as soon as that was over they would go and hunt to pay their debts. After black drink I set out with Mr. Forest and my Servant to the Worsitas, where I went to the Square where Salegee and some others were at black drink. We Stayed with them untill our horses and baggage were got aCross the Chatahutchie River, and about Eleven Oclock proceeded on our Journey, taking the Course and distance of the path as we went along; at a Branch of a Creek (which joins the River opposite Eutchie) Called the twelve mile branch, we came up to one Howarth, a half breed Indian who was waiting for us on purpose to go to Charles Town to see his Father. We proceeded on to another Branch of this Creek where we Encamped all night. (Taitt, quoted in Mereness 1916: 560)

---

flood of settlers. Friction between the Creeks and their hereditary enemies, the Cherokees, continued as the Cherokees expanded southward and westward. They apparently displaced the Creeks in northern Georgia before contact with the English, for the Creeks still claimed this part of the state by right of original possession. According to legend, these two groups fought in the battle of Taliwa about 1755, apparently somewhere near the present town of Canton (Cherokee County). The Cherokees won a decisive victory, and the Creeks abandoned this part of the state (see Mooney 1900: 384–85). One of the stories of the origin of the name of

Blood Mountain is also related to the Creek and Cherokee contest for north Georgia. According to tradition, the two tribes fought a major battle on this mountain, and so many were killed that the streams flowing from the mountain ran red with blood.

The French and Indian War affected Georgia little. At the outset of hostilities in 1754, the Cherokees favored the French because of the increasing pressure on the borders by the land-hungry English settlers and because of unscrupulous traders who consistently cheated the Indians. However, the English were closer and could make their military power felt much more easily than could the French. With the British victory and the elimination of the French threat, an uneasy situation prevailed until the beginning of the American Revolution. Angered by continuing encroachments on their land and by persistent problems with traders from the colonies, the Cherokees were easily persuaded to support the British in quelling the revolt. They attacked all along the frontier in Georgia and the Carolinas, prompting military forces from these areas to retaliate. In July 1776, a force of some two hundred men entered the Cherokee portion of Georgia, burning towns and destroying crops along the headwaters of the Chattahoochee and Tugalo Rivers. Similar expeditions were mounted in the Carolinas and Virginia, and the result was a crippling blow to the Cherokees.

As late as 1782, John Sevier led a small army against the Chickamauga band of Cherokees, destroying towns on Chickamauga Creek and penetrating as far as the headwaters of the Coosa River in northwest Georgia. James Mooney describes the Cherokees' situation at the close of the Revolution: "By seven years of constant warfare they had been reduced to the lowest depth of misery, almost indeed to the verge of extinction. Over and over again their towns had been laid in ashes and their fields wasted. Their best warriors had been killed and their women and children had sickened and starved in the mountains. Their great war chief, Oconostota, who had led them to victory in 1780, was now a broken old man. . . . To complete their brimming cup of misery the smallpox again broke out among them in 1783. Deprived of the assistance of their former white allies they were left to their own cruel fate" (1900: 61). By the Treaty of Augusta in 1783, the Cherokee ceded more land to the United States, including a portion of northeast Georgia that would become Franklin County.

Creeks in Georgia in the years before the revolution were in a somewhat different position. They, too, felt the pressure of white greed for land, but they became rather adept at dealing with the Spanish, French, and English. As one after another of the European powers was eliminated from the Southeast, the Creeks were left with primarily the English and the American settlers on the eve of the American Revolution. When the war began, the Creeks were divided; some favored supporting the British, a few favored the American side, and some advised a neutral position. With the American victory, the westward push continued, and by the Treaties of Augusta in 1783, Galphinton in 1785, and Shoulderbone in 1786, the Creeks lost more land in Georgia.

Cultural change among the Indian tribes had accelerated in the years before the American Revolution, a trend that would continue in the decades between the end of the war and the Removal. Even before the revolution, according to James Adair, "The Indians, by reason of our supplying them so cheap with every sort of goods, have forgotten the chief part of their ancient mechanical skill, so as not to be well able now, at least for some years, to live independent of us" ([1930] 1974: 456).

Suggestions for Further Reading

Adair, James. [1930] 1974. *Adair's History of the American Indians,* ed. Samuel Cole Williams. New York: Promontory Press.

Clayton, Lawrence A., Vernon James Knight, Jr., and Edward C. Moore, eds. 1993. *The De Soto Chronicles: The Expedition of Hernando de Soto to North America in 1539–1543.* Vol. 1. Tuscaloosa: University of Alabama Press.

Hudson, Charles, and Carmen Chaves Tesser, eds. 1994. *The Forgotten Centuries: Indians and Europeans in the American South, 1521–1704.* Athens: University of Georgia Press.

Smith, Marvin T. 1987. *Archaeology of Aboriginal Culture Change in the Interior Southeast: Depopulation during the Early Historic Period.* Gainesville: University Press of Florida.

Swanton, John R. [1922] 1998. *Early History of the Creek Indians and Their Neighbors.* Reprint, Gainesville: University Press of Florida.

7

The Historic Tribes

In the first clearing of their plantations, they only bark the large timber, cut down the saplings and underwood, and burn them in heaps; as the suckers shoot up, they chop them off close to the stump, of which they make fires to deaden the roots, till in time they decay. Though, to a stranger, this may seem to be a lazy method of clearing the wood-lands; yet it is the most expeditious method they could have pitched upon, under their circumstances, as a common hoe and a small hatchet are all their implements for clearing and planting.

—James Adair, in Swanton, *Indians of the Southeastern United States,* 304

During the early historic period, the area of what is now Georgia was home to many tribes of Native Americans, each with its distinctive culture. In many instances, there was considerable continuity from the prehistoric period into the historic period, for both the historical record and archaeological discoveries agree. A case in point is the economic system: The agricultural way of life became established in Georgia and the greater Southeast after A.D. 1000, but the older hunting-fishing-gathering cycle continued in an important but secondary role. This way of life characterized the tribes encountered by the Spanish, English, and French as they moved inland from their coastal settlements; these early explorers, traders, missionaries, and military personnel were not anthropologists, and their accounts of Indian life are incomplete at best. By the time anthropology came into being as a scientific discipline, Georgia was devoid of its native population, and the survivors of the Georgia tribes had changed drastically in their new home in Oklahoma.

The historic tribes of Georgia, similar in some ways, diverse in others, knew the mountains and hills, the rivers and swamps, better than we do. Many features of the natural landscape, as well as some of our cities and counties, bear names that link them to Georgia's native tribes. Although the people are gone, their memory and their mark on the land and on Georgia's history remain.

The Creeks

Perhaps you have wondered what Georgia was like when the first Europeans appeared on the scene. Certainly the forest cover would have differed: The natural landscape would have had trees of gigantic proportions clothing all of Georgia, with different species dominating in different parts of the state. Rivers and streams ran clear and deep and were not full of silt as they often are today. Game was abundant. But we want to examine the cultural landscape, so let us look at the Creek Indians, who claimed most of Georgia as their home.

There are several versions accounting for the origin of the tribal name. One story says that as the English traders made their way inland from the coast, they found that most of the streams flowed from north to south. Since they were traveling westward, they had to cross one creek after another, so they came to refer to the Indian groups living along these streams as "Creeks." A more likely account has to do with the Charleston settlement. According to this version, the English traders established friendly relations with an Indian settlement on Ocheese Creek (Ocmulgee River). The traders referred to the group as the Ocheese Creek Indians. Later, they dropped the word "Ocheese" and expanded the usage of "Creek Indians" to all Indians who spoke a similar language and had a similar culture to those they knew.

However they came to be known collectively, the Creek Indians were a rather diverse group made up of numerous small tribes or bands, all speaking related languages and sharing a similar culture. The dominant group is called the Muskogee, and it was composed of twelve bands: Kasihta, Coweta, Coosa, Abihka, Wakokai, Eufaula, Hilibi, Atasi, Kolomi, Tukabahchee, Pakana, and Okchai. In time, the groups living along the Coosa, Tallapoosa, and Alabama Rivers came to be called the Upper Creeks, and those living along the Flint and lower Chattahoochee Rivers were called the Lower Creeks. The languages they spoke were all part of the Muskogean language family, which includes the languages of the Choctaw, Chickasaw, and others.

In keeping with the settlement pattern established in Mississippian times, Creek villages were situated along the rivers of their territory. There were several reasons for this pattern. Rivers were arteries of communication, for considerable travel in dugout canoes apparently took place. Also the rich alluvial soil of the bottomlands was ideal for agriculture: it was free of stones and was relatively easy to clear (vast canebrakes covering the bottomlands in many areas could be cleared by burning). The native people had no metal tools until they acquired them from the Europeans. Until then, their only agricultural implements were digging sticks and stone or bone hoes. Another reason for locating villages in the river bottoms was their access to several ecological zones. Hunting and gathering remained important, and the river provided a variety of food resources. The surrounding bottomlands and swamps had other resources, and the uplands had still other plants and animals to be exploited.

We know from early historic descriptions that Creek villages had many features reminiscent of Mississippian centers. Consisting of houses numbering from thirty to a hundred or more, these settlements were strung out along the rivers, with more density around the ceremonial center. Villages in border areas were more compact and were fortified against raids. William Bartram, a botanist who traveled in Georgia and Florida in the mid-1700s, described the habitations of the Alachua (Oconee) as having

two houses nearly the same size about thirty feet in length, twelve feet wide, and about the same in height. The door is placed midway on one side or in the front. This house is divided equally, across, into two apartments, one of which is the cook room. The other house is nearly of the same dimensions, standing about twenty yards from the dwelling house, its end fronting the door. The building is two stories high and constructed in a different manner. It is divided transversely, as the other, but the end next the dwelling house is open on three sides, supported by posts or pillars. It has an open loft or platform, the ascent to which is by a portable stair or ladder: this is a pleasant, cool, airy situation, and here the master or chief of the family retires to repose in the hot seasons, and receives his guests or visitors. The other half of this building is closed on all sides by notched logs; the lowest or ground part is a potatoe house, and the upper story over it is a granary for corn and other provisions. Their houses are constructed of a kind of frame. In the first place, strong corner pillars are fixed in the ground, with others somewhat less, ranging on a line between; these are strengthened by cross pieces of timber, and the whole with the roof is covered close with the bark of the Cypress tree. (Bartram [1928] 1955: 168)

Although Bartram observed these dwellings in north Florida, they seem to be typical of Creek practice throughout the region. Each Creek town had a ceremonial center that contained a rotunda, a circular building used for large meetings at which participants were seated according to rank. This building was of wattle-and-daub construction, with a roof of pine bark, and its entrance was on the east or south side. Opposite this building was a yard where the popular game chunkey was played. Here also, poles were erected, one of which bore the town emblem. The other poles were sometimes the scene of the torture and burning of war captives.

Of the Creeks' physical appearance, Bartram said that the women were "remarkably short of stature," well-proportioned, and attractive. He described the men as tall and with a darker complexion than that of other southeastern tribes. Their darker skin might have resulted from exposure to the sun, for General Oglethorpe recorded that the Indians around Savannah anointed themselves with oil and exposed themselves to the sun. Oglethorpe went on to say that the Indian men used red, blue, yellow, and black paints to decorate themselves. Clothing for the men consisted of a breechclout; women wore a skirt that reached to the knees.

A few years after Oglethorpe recorded these descriptions, Bartram wrote that Creek men wore a linen shirt, breechclout, cloth leggings, and moccasins. At that time, in the mid-eighteenth century, it was the custom for Creek men to shave their heads, leaving a narrow crest of hair begin-

---

Most of the Indians have clean, neat, dwelling houses, white-washed within and without, either with decayed oyster-shells, coarse-chalk, or white marly clay; one or other of which, each of our Indian nations abounds with, be they ever so far distant from the sea-shore: the Indians, as well as the traders, usually decorate their summer-houses with this favourite white-wash. The former have likewise each a corn-house, fowl-house, and a hot-house, or stove for winter: and so have the traders likewise separate store-houses for their goods, as well as to contain the proper remittances received in exchange. (Adair [1930] 1974: 443)

Fig. 7.1. Yoholo-mico, a Creek Indian (courtesy of Hargrett Rare Book and Manuscript Library/University of Georgia Libraries)

ning at the top of the head and gradually widening toward the back; the hair remaining at the back of the head and neck was allowed to grow long and was decorated with pendants and feathers. Creek men also wore a band about four inches wide around their heads. Bartram recorded that this band was decorated with stones, beads, and other items, and a peak in the front was embellished with a long plume of crane or heron feathers (Bartram 1955:393). He described the women as wearing a short waist-coat and a skirt, their hair plaited and fastened at the crown of the head with a silver brooch. On ceremonial or festive occasions, the women decorated their hair with long ribbons of many colors.

The Creeks, like other southeastern tribes, were matrilineal, which meant that women occupied an important and influential position in society. Typically, women were the property owners, and inheritance was through the female line. Clan membership, one of the most important elements in Creek society, was inherited matrilineally, that is, one belonged to one's mother's clan. Clan affiliation determined to a great extent one's position in society, for some clans were considered more important, and thus more powerful, than others. The Creeks had about fifty clans, among them the Wind, Bear, Fox, Alligator, Cane, Arrow, Beaver, Panther, Wolf, Salt, and Corn clans.

The governmental structure of the Creek Indians was based in the *talwa* (town), which resembled the political and religious centers of the Mississippian time period in that it included the town itself along with outlying villages and settlements. Populations in Creek towns ranged from about a hundred to a thousand or more. This tribe exhibited what anthropologists refer to as a moiety system, a twofold division of society. Towns, clans, and even the territory controlled by the Creeks demonstrated this feature, for all were divided into Red (war) and White (peace) organizations or divisions. While every town was known as either a Red town or a White town, each town had a Red chief and a White chief, the Red chief assuming leadership during time of war, the White chief presiding at other times. A *miko* (chief) had numerous duties, and Bartram said of the White chief, "He has the disposal of the corn and fruits, and gives audience to ambassadors, deputies, and strangers who come to the town or tribe, receives presents, etc." (quoted in Swanton 1928: 278).

The White chief served as head and spokesman for the tribal council. He was assisted in his duties by a vice-chief and a group of lesser chiefs representing the various clans. Red towns were associated with war, and the duties of the Red chief "consisted in directing all of the war operations, in taking all measures necessary to revenge an injury inflicted on the nation and in defending its rights. He was invested with authority sufficient for this purpose; . . . once peace was reestablished and the troops returned . . . he again became a plain citizen" (Milfort, quoted in Swanton 1928:298).

Creek ceremonial life was marked by several important occasions throughout the year. One of the most important was the great Busk, or Boskita, Ceremony. Also called the Green Corn Ceremony, it was held in midsummer and marked the beginning of a new year. The ceremony involved feasting, dancing, a stickball game, and the New Fire Ceremony. For the New Fire Ceremony, four logs were cut and brought to the square-ground. All fires in the town were extinguished, and utensils used in cook-

ing over the old fires were broken. A new fire was kindled in the square-
ground by a priest, and the four logs were placed in this fire as offerings.
Afterward, coals from the new fire were used to kindle household fires
throughout the town. It was sometime after this that the "black drink"
was taken. Made from plants, this powerful emetic was vomited shortly
after it was drunk. Believed to purify the mind and body, it was an important part of Creek life and was noted by their European visitors.

We have only incomplete knowledge of the ceremonies and practices of
the Creeks at points in what anthropologists call the life cycle: birth, pu-
berty, marriage, and death. We do know that Creek women retired to a
special house to give birth, where the new mother was attended by other
women. This house was constructed at some distance from the rest of the

---

The Creek busk, certainly the most impressive ceremonial in the entire Southeast, was in all probability derived from the old rectangular
townhouse ceremonial. In fact, evidence has been presented suggesting
that the busk represents the clearest survival of mound ceremonial
and that several elements of the busk refer to mound-building activity.

Creek religion possessed features which suggest Cult survivals.
In the first place, in the new-fire ceremonial it had a spectacular ritual
associated with a performance which exacted a year-round and all-
prevailing religious duty, namely tending the new fire in the individual
dwellings and seeing that it was properly extinguished before the next
busk. It possessed a group of ethical concepts (peace, expiation of sin,
etc.) of a type which in their demands on the individual have commonly been associated with cult phenomena throughout the world.
These again exacted a standard of personal behavior for the welfare
of the entire group. It served as a communal ritual in which all members of the group except "criminals" participated and was intimately
related to communal agriculture and the communal consumption of
the crop. In the possession of elaborate religious structures located in
ceremonial centers, it provided points of social focus and thus served
as a powerful cohesive force in a scattered population, which by the
nature of its basic economy, could be no more concentrated. (Waring
1968: 63)

---

settlement, because it was believed that the blood and fluids associated with childbirth were polluting and dangerous, particularly to men. The woman had to remain in this house for four days, during which she used her own dishes and other utensils reserved for these times. After giving birth, she had to bathe and change her clothes. The newborn infant was immediately plunged into cold water. As the child was growing up, it was never whipped or slapped but, if punishment or correction was necessary, the individual was scratched by the mother with a pin, needle, or the sharp teeth in a garfish jaw.

During their monthly menstrual cycle, girls were confined to the house built apart from the settlement, for many of the beliefs about the fluids associated with childbirth also applied to the menstrual fluids. Before marriage, Creek girls were allowed sexual freedom, but after marriage, adultery was regarded as a serious matter and was severely punished.

Marriages among the Creeks took place when the woman was "bound" to her husband by a payment to the bride's family. The prospective husband also gave presents to the intended bride and helped her work in the cornfields. Benjamin Hawkins noted that "when a man has built a house, made his crop, and gathered it in, then made his hunt and brought home the meat, and put all this in the possession of his wife, the ceremony ends, and they are married" (quoted in Swanton 1946: 704).

At death, it was apparently the Creek custom to wrap the body in a blanket and bury it in a flexed position. At the death of a prominent man, green tree branches were hung in the square-ground. A widower was expected to mourn and remain celibate for four months after the death of his wife, but a widow had the same observance extended to four years. However, she could be released from this obligation by the relatives of her deceased husband.

As did other tribes in the Southeast, the Creeks practiced agriculture on a rather intensive basis but continued to supplement agricultural produce by hunting, fishing, and gathering. Apparently, they planted small garden plots near each household. Larger fields located farther away were worked cooperatively, and a portion of the harvest was stored in a public granary under control of the chief, who saw to it that needy families were supplied with food from this facility. He might also draw upon this source to help other towns whose crops were destroyed or lost, or to supply war parties. Wild foods used by the Creeks included persimmons, mulberries, hickory nuts, acorns, grapes, and honey-locust pods. Early visitors among the Creeks noted that they ate deer, bear, turkey, freshwater turtle, fish, and small game. All of this meant that the Creeks could survive even in the event of a crop failure. With increasing white contact, however, new crops and farming techniques were introduced, game was depleted as a result of the skin trade, and former hunting lands were given up to the increasing flood of white settlers.

The French of West-Florida, and the English colonists, got from the Indians different sorts of beans and peas, with which they were before entirely unacquainted. And they plant a sort of small tobacco, which the French and English have not. All the Indian nations we have any acquaintance with, frequently use it on the most religious occasions. The women plant also pompions, and different sorts of melons, in separate fields, at a considerable distance from the town, where each owner raises an high scaffold, to over-look this favourite part of their vegetable possessions: and though the enemy sometimes kills them in this their strict watch duty, yet it is a very rare thing to pass by those fields, without seeing them there at watch. This usually is the duty of the old women, who fret at the very shadow of a crow, when he chances to pass on his wide survey of the fields; but if pinching hunger should excite him to descend, they soon frighten him away with their screeches. When the pompions are ripe, they cut them into long circling slices, which they barbacue, or dry with a slow heat. And when they have half boiled the larger sort of potatoes, they likewise dry them over a moderate fire, and chiefly use them in the spring-season, mixt with their favourite bear's oil. As soon as the larger sort of corn is full-eared, they half-boil it too, and dry it either by the sun, or over a slow fire; which might be done, as well, in a moderately hot oven, if the heat was renewed as occasion required. This they boil with venison, or any other unsalted flesh. They commonly have pretty good crops, which is owing to the richness of the soil. . . . They plant their corn in straight rows, putting five or six grains into one hole, about two inches distant—They cover them with clay in the form of a small hill. Each row is a yard asunder, and in the vacant ground they plant pumpkins, water-melons, marsh-mallows, sun-flowers, and sundry sorts of beans and peas, the last two of which yield a large increase. (Adair [1930] 1974: 438–39)

The Cherokees

The northernmost portion of Georgia was occupied by the Cherokees, a tribe that evidently originated to the north and moved southward through the mountains during the late prehistoric period. The Cherokee language belongs to the Iroquoian linguistic family and is thus not related to the languages of the Creeks or other peoples in Georgia. Most Iroquoian speakers were located in the New York–Pennsylvania–Ontario area, and this location along with tribal legends points to a more northern origin for the Cherokees (see Mooney 1900). Their expansion southward meant the displacement of other peoples; the Creeks were still being pushed out of north Georgia during the early historic period. The Cherokees formed the largest tribal group east of the Mississippi, and their geographic location at the southern terminus of the Appalachians enhanced their significance in the early history of the United States.

Like the Creeks and other tribes of the Southeast, the Cherokees lived by farming and by hunting, fishing, and gathering. Their villages lay in the bottomlands along the rivers in the northernmost part of the state. In 1776, William Bartram described a Cherokee town: "All before me and on every side, appeared little plantations of young Corn, Beans, etc. divided from each other by narrow strips or borders of grass, which marked the bounds of each one's property, their habitation standing in the midst" (Bartram 1955: 284). Concerning individual dwellings, Bartram says: "The Cherokee construct their habitations on a different plan from the Creeks; that is, but one oblong four square building, of one story high; the materials consisting of logs or trunks of trees, stripped of their bark, notched at their ends, fixed one upon another, and afterwards plaistered well, both inside and out, with clay tempered with dry grass, and the whole covered or roofed with the bark of the chestnut tree or long broad shingles" (296). As in the case of the Creeks, towns near the border with another tribe were more compact and were fortified against raids.

The Cherokees are described as lighter skinned and taller than the Creeks, the women tall and "of a delicate frame" (Bartram 1955: 380). Cherokee men shaved their heads, leaving only a scalp lock on the top or back. This they decorated with beads, feathers, and other items. Paintings of Cherokees dating from the early and mid-eighteenth century show them dressed in items of clothing obtained from traders. Somewhat later, the turban and other accoutrements became fashionable. In earlier times,

Fig. 7.2. Too-an-Tuh, a Cherokee Indian (courtesy of Hargrett Rare Book and Manuscript Library/University of Georgia Libraries)

men wore a breechclout, buckskin leggings, moccasins, and a buckskin shirt. Women wore a buckskin skirt, and both men and women wore a cloth garment similar to a toga. Women also fashioned skirts from strips of the bark of mulberry roots or wove cloth for skirts from the fiber of wild hemp. Another garment must have been beautiful to behold, for it was made from the iridescent feathers of the wild turkey. For this, the ends of the feathers were sewn between two strips of mulberry bark, and the strips probably arranged on a cloth foundation to make a skirt or cape.

Cherokee society, like that of the Creeks, was matrilineal, and women occupied a prominent and important place. Their position is indicated by the fact that some became warriors, and others were powerful in tribal councils. A woman active in the council was referred to as a "Beloved Woman" or "Honored Woman." In 1785, it is recorded that the "War Woman of Chota" addressed the treaty conference at Hopewell. Women controlled much of the economic life of the Cherokees, and property was inherited through the female line.

The Cherokees also had Red and White organizations, but these differed somewhat from the Creek moieties. Among the Cherokees, the White organization was roughly equivalent to our civil authority, while the Red organization furnished what we would call martial law. Each organization had its own officials and its own functions. The White organization was in charge during times of peace. Each town had a White chief, but the White chief of the capital town was regarded as the paramount chief. If a White chief died suddenly or unexpectedly, his wife could assume the duties of the office until a successor was installed. White organization officials "alone possessed prayers for invoking the sun and moon and other protective spirits who could take away disease and ill health. They could separate the unclean elements from polluted persons and restore the normal condition. Their persons and belongings were sacred and were not like ordinary citizens and their possessions. The sacredness of the white officials was so great as to separate them as a class superior to the rest of the community and in some respects above the ordinary laws and usages" (Gilbert 1943:357).

The Red organization assumed leadership during time of war. Each town had a war chief, a great war captain who was elected by the warriors subject to approval by the White chief. Magical procedures and purification rites were carried out before and after war expeditions to ensure success.

The ceremonial life of the Cherokees centered on observances of lunar phases or stages in the growing season. They believed that the world had been created in autumn, and with the new moon in October they observed the beginning of a new year. An important ceremony took place in the spring, a major part of which involved the chief of the town, who gazed into a sacred quartz crystal and, on the basis of what he saw, predicted whether there would be a good crop. At the Green Corn Ceremony in midsummer, seven ears of corn were offered in the fire, each from the field of a different clan. Christian missionary activity eventually led to the end of most of the ceremonies and dances, and little is known of the tribe's traditional religious beliefs. From what is known, it is apparent that the Cherokees believed in a Supreme Being who was a unity of three separate beings called the "Elder Fires Above." It was believed that these beings had created the sun, moon, and earth but had left the sun and moon to create the stars and all living things.

Perhaps the most important aspect of Cherokee society was the clan system. Clan membership was matrilineal, and each clan was represented in every Cherokee town. The Cherokees had seven clans, among them the Bird, Deer, Paint, and Wolf clans. As among the Creeks, clan membership determined one's civic and ceremonial duties and to a certain extent limited one's choice of a marriage partner. Members of the same clan were forbidden to marry, and one could not marry into a clan that stood in a particular relationship to his or hers.

The life cycle for the Cherokees was marked by ceremonies and the observance of taboos. A woman gave birth in a separate house, attended by older women. The medicine man was the only male permitted to be present, and then only for a difficult delivery. As soon as the baby was born, it was dipped into water, an act repeated every morning for two years. During her pregnancy, the woman was subjected to numerous restrictions and was taken to a river or creek at each new moon for at least three months before giving birth. It was at the river or creek that a priest performed rituals to ensure a healthy child, an easy delivery, and other positive outcomes.

Marriage involved payment of a bride price, a transfer of goods from the groom to his intended in-laws. If accepted, according to some accounts, there was a public ceremony that involved feasting and a symbolic exchange of gifts of food between bride and groom. This is said to have symbolized the division of labor between man and woman in the household, the groom having presented the bride some venison, while she gave him some corn.

In historic times, the Cherokees buried their dead on the slope of a hill. Before the burial, neighbors gathered, and in more recent times hymns were sung all night. Medicine men avoided these procedures for ritual reasons. After the burial, the old ashes from the fireplace were scattered over the yard of the house where the deceased had lived (see Swanton 1946:724).

The Cherokees grew corn, pumpkins, beans, and other crops and readily adopted plants brought by the English, so that by the mid-eighteenth century they were growing melons, peas, and other crops. They also had orchards of fruit trees, which were destroyed by the military expeditions against the Cherokees in 1776. The agricultural produce was supplemented by wild foods such as chestnuts, acorns, hickory nuts, walnuts, blackberries, wild strawberries, and numerous other plant foods. In addition, fish and turtles were important resources, and deer and bear furnished most of the meat supply. Smaller game supplemented this list: Squirrels, birds, and other small creatures were killed by means of a blowgun. The way of life of the Cherokees would be irrevocably altered in the years following the American Revolution, although the Eastern Band of Cherokees would continue to use some of these food sources down to the present time.

Other Tribes

The small coastal tribes, along with the more numerous Timucua, discussed earlier, disappeared at an early date, their remnants migrating to join the Spaniards at St. Augustine or being absorbed by other groups, particularly the Creeks. But other small tribal groups also played a role in Georgia's early history. Among these, one of the most prominent is the Yuchi (pronounced "Yoo-chee"). Calling themselves Tsoyaha, or "Offspring of the Sun," they appear to have lived in or near the Blue Ridge Mountains. In early historic times, they moved south, with one group settling on the Savannah River near the present site of Augusta. Others settled lower on the Savannah, and eventually most or all of the Yuchi moved to the lower Chattahoochee and settled among the Creeks. William Bartram described a Yuchi town on the Chattahoochee as follows:

> Situated in a vast plain . . . on the gradual ascent as we rise from a narrow strip of low ground immediately bordering on the river: it is the largest, most compact, and best situated Indian town I ever saw; the habitations are large and neatly built; the walls of the houses are constructed of a wooden frame, then lathed and plaistered inside and out with a reddish well tempered clay or mortar . . . and these houses are neatly covered or roofed with Cypress bark or shingles of that tree. (1955: 312)

In the historic period, the Yuchi dressed in a manner similar to that of neighboring tribes, men in brightly colored calico shirts under sleeved jackets that reached their knees. Men also wore breechclouts, leggings, moccasins, and turbans decorated with feathers. Yuchi women wore calico dresses ornamented with silver brooches and a beaded belt. On ceremonial occasions, they wore large, curved, ornate combs in their hair, from which ribbons of various colors streamed to the ground (see Speck 1909:46).

Benjamin Hawkins noted that the Yuchi were "more civil and orderly" than the Creeks, and that they retained their own distinct customs even though they were living among the Creeks. He also mentioned that "the men take part of the labors of the women, and are more constant in their attachment to their women than is usual among red people" (1848: 62).

Two male organizations, the Chief society and the Warrior society, regulated Yuchi life. Equivalent to the White and Red organizations of the Creeks, the two societies had both civil and ceremonial functions. Town chiefs, priests, and ceremonial leaders were chosen from the most important of the clans, the Bear, Wolf, Tortoise, and Deer. These and the other clans were matrilineal.

Like other tribes in the area, the Yuchi practiced agriculture and hunting, fishing, and gathering. Speck noted that "almost any kind of bird, animal, or fish that was large enough to bother with was used as food" (1909: 45). Since agriculture furnished a significant portion of their food, they observed the Green Corn Ceremony, during which the New Fire ritual was performed. The black drink was also a part of this important ceremony, which ended with a feast and a ball game.

Other tribal groups represented in Georgia in the Early Historic Period included the Shawnee and Chickasaw. The Shawnee settlements were mostly along the Cumberland River in Tennessee and Kentucky, but in the late seventeenth century a band moved to the Savannah River near Augusta. By 1708, there were three Shawnee towns there. After the ill-fated Yamassee War, these Shawnee groups began to disintegrate, some moving to Pennsylvania to join other Indian groups there, others to the lower Chattahoochee River, where they lived among the Creeks. Apparently, this latter group left the Creek country before the Removal, but friendship between the Creeks and Shawnees persisted.

Chickasaw territory was in northeastern Mississippi, but in 1737 a band founded a town near the newly established trading post at Augusta. They evidently remained there until the American Revolution began, at which time they rejoined the main Chickasaw settlements.

Suggestions for Further Reading

Gilbert, William H., Jr. 1943. *The Eastern Cherokees*. Bureau of American Ethnology Bulletin 133, Anthropological Papers 23. Washington: Government Printing Office.
Hawkins, Benjamin. 1848. *A Sketch of the Creek Country in 1798 and 1799*. Georgia Historical Society Collections, vol. 3, pt. 1.
Swanton, John R. 1946. *Indians of the Southeastern United States*. Bureau of American Ethnology Bulletin 137. Washington: Government Printing Office.

8

What Happened

Oh! Christians, pray for the Cherokees—Oppression scowls about their borders.

—Rev. Evan Jones, July 28, 1830, in Gardner,
Cherokees and Baptists in Georgia, 118–19

How do we explain why Georgia has no native tribes today? While many of the smaller tribes, particularly the coastal groups, either became extinct or were absorbed by other groups, the larger tribes persisted in the interior. As the larger tribes struggled to hold on to their ancestral lands, the governments of Georgia and the United States were determined to rid the state of its original inhabitants and open their land for white settlement. The various treaties and resulting land cessions clearly demonstrate the erosion of native lands from tribal control.

The years following the American Revolution witnessesd increasing attention to Georgia's Indians. Some people sought to civilize them by converting them to Christianity. Others, particularly the government, merely wanted to get rid of them, however this might be effected. It is easy for us to condemn the actions of state and national officials for their handling of Indian affairs, but it must be remembered that times were different. Rather than judge the past by today's standards, we should learn from it. This is not to lessen the condemnation of the dishonesty, hypocrisy, and downright cruelty displayed by government leaders toward the Indian peoples. What follows is a brief summary of the events leading up to the expulsion of the Creeks and Cherokees from Georgia.

The Creek Story

At the Treaty of Augusta in May 1783, the Georgians induced a few Creek leaders to sign a document that called for them to give up some favorite Creek hunting grounds between the Tugalo and Oconee Rivers. The Creek national council refused to ratify this "treaty," but the government of Georgia nevertheless proceeded to divide the land into counties and open it for white settlement. Disputes between Georgia and the Creeks continued until 1790, when a treaty called for the Creeks to cede more land but guaranteed to protect the remaining Creek lands in Georgia from any further encroachment by whites. Border troubles continued, however, mostly instigated by white troublemakers who sneaked into Creek territory to murder and steal.

Under increasing pressure from the flood of settlers, the Creeks sold more land to the federal government, including a tract between the Oconee and Ocmulgee Rivers in 1802. In the same year, Georgia and the U.S. government reached an agreement concerning Georgia's claim to all the land westward to the Mississippi River. Under the agreement, the federal government purchased the state's claim to what would later become Alabama and Mississippi and agreed to eradicate Indian titles to all land within Georgia's new boundaries as soon as it could be done in a peaceable manner. In 1805, more land was obtained from the Creeks, who further agreed to the construction of a road across their land. This road was to be complete with ferries and inns. One of the Creeks who agreed to this treaty was the mixed blood William McIntosh.

In 1813, the Shawnee leader, Tecumseh, enlisted a portion of the Creeks in his proposed confederacy of tribes to halt white encroachment. This move precipitated the war of 1813–14, which ended in the disastrous battle at Horseshoe Bend, Alabama. Andrew Jackson, who commanded the American troops, now required the Creeks to relinquish 22 million acres of land in central and southern Alabama and south Georgia. The Creeks found themselves in an increasingly perplexing and dangerous situation, as crimes committed against them by whites went unpunished. Some leaders requested that teachers come among them so that they could begin to adjust to a more European life-style. Accordingly, some schools were established, and missionaries, particularly Baptists and Methodists, became active among the Creeks.

In 1821, a treaty session was held at Indian Springs (Butts County) which resulted in the Creeks selling the whites 5 million acres between the

Fig. 8.1. Opothle-yoholo, a Creek leader (courtesy of Hargrett Rare
Book and Manuscript Library/University of Georgia Libraries)

Ocmulgee and Flint Rivers. William McIntosh was one of the prominent
speakers at this session, favoring the deal. Despite all the land acquisi-
tions, however, Georgia officials were still urging the Creeks to exchange
the remainder of their land for land in the West. In 1825, another meeting
was announced, this one to be held at McIntosh's inn at Indian Springs.
The treaty under consideration provided for the sale of all remaining
Creek land in Georgia, plus a vast tract in northern Alabama, plus the
awarding of land in the West. Despite the eloquent opposition of Opothle-

yoholo, McIntosh and a few others signed the treaty. The Creek council, which had decreed that anyone agreeing to more land cessions would be executed, ordered McIntosh's death. Acting on this order, about a hundred Creeks led by Menawa surrounded McIntosh's home in what is now Carroll County. Allowing the women and children to leave, the warriors then set fire to the house. When McIntosh attempted to flee the burning building, he was shot down.

The less progressive inhabitants of the ceded territory crossed the Chattahoochee and joined their brethren in Alabama. An English traveler who visited the new agency at Fort Mitchell in the spring of 1828 gave an unforgettable description of "those miserable wretches who had been dislodged from their ancient territory" and were "wandering about like bees whose hive has been destroyed." Crowell was distributing clothing and food, but many had starved to death.

A great contrast to these despairing refugees was presented by the enterprising settlers who hastened to occupy the territory they had abandoned. Georgia had disposed of the land by lottery in the summer of 1827, and the speculative fervor of her citizens was raised to fever pitch. A townsite on the Chattahoochee had been reserved for the future city of Columbus, and it was planned to advertise the lots to prospective buyers throughout the United States. Four months before the time set for the lot sale, this English visitor found about nine hundred people assembled on the site hoping to secure an advantage through possession. One of these "inhabitants" proudly conducted him over the "city." As they followed the "principle street"—a lane cut through the living forest—they heard anvils "ringing away merrily at every corner; while saws, axes, and hammers were seen flashing amongst the woods all around." Many of the houses were built on wheels to be moved to a permanent location as soon as the lots should be offered for sale. Another English traveler who visited the place a bare two years later found a thriving town of fifteen hundred people, three churches, a post office, several brick buildings, and many comfortable frame houses. Truly the American frontier was an irresistible force rolling on to destroy the Creeks. (Debo 1941: 95–96)

After this action, a Creek delegation was called to Washington. The delegation refused to negotiate until the McIntosh treaty had been repudiated by the government. However, intense pressure from the Georgia government forced the Creeks to cede all their remaining land in Georgia except a small tract north of the Chattahoochee River. Even this small tract was given up under pressure, and Georgia was rid of the Creeks at last, or so the government thought. The first accurate survey of the state's western boundary revealed that a small portion of the state remained in Creek hands. This was obtained shortly, and, as Debo remarks, "The expulsion of the Creeks from the soil of Georgia was now complete. Less than a century had passed since they had welcomed Oglethorpe to the gracious abundance of their towns" (1941: 95).

The Creeks were now Alabama's problem and would soon be conducted to Indian Territory in the West under the federal government's Indian removal program. Georgia was left with the Cherokees.

The Cherokee Story

In the years following the American Revolution, efforts to "civilize" the Cherokees intensified. This was particularly the case after 1791, when a

Fig. 8.2. Fort Hollingsworth/White House, a frontier fort dating from 1793, Banks County (courtesy Friends of the Fort)

treaty provided for furnishing the Cherokees with the latest farming tools and other items. In 1801, Benjamin Hawkins wrote that spinning wheels, looms, and ploughs were in general use among the Cherokees, who displayed considerable interest in farming, manufacturing, and raising livestock. In that year and the years following, Christian missionaries, chiefly representing the Moravians, Baptists, and Presbyterians, began work among the Cherokees. At the request of some tribal leaders, the Moravians established a school at Spring Place (Murray County) in 1801.

In the War of 1812, the Cherokees contributed several hundred warriors to the forces led by General Andrew Jackson, and these Cherokees were instrumental in bringing about the defeat of the Creeks at Horseshoe Bend. This aid would not dissuade the government from its goal: dispossessing the Cherokees and removing them to west of the Mississippi.

In the fall of 1820, the Cherokees formed a government patterned after that of the United States. The national legislature was composed of an upper and a lower house, with members elected by the voters in each district. Each district held council meetings twice a year, and each had a judge and a marshal. Missions and their schools were flourishing, one superintendent reporting that Cherokee children were "apt to learn, willing to labor, and readily submissive to discipline" (Mooney 1900: 108).

In 1821, Sequoyah, a Cherokee, made public his phenomenal invention: a way to write the Cherokee language by using symbols to represent the sounds. Sequoyah demonstrated to the tribal council how it worked, and the council adopted the syllabary. "On account of the remarkable adaptation of the syllabary to the language, it was only necessary to learn the characters to be able to read at once" (Mooney 1900: 110). The syllabary is the more remarkable for its invention when we realize that Sequoyah was an illiterate man. For years, he had wanted to emulate the white's ability to convey messages by making marks on paper. His desire to commit the Indian language to writing led him to experiment over a period of years until he came up with a method of devising a symbol to represent a sound. In 1824, a portion of St. John's Gospel was translated and hundreds of copies made and circulated throughout the nation. In the next year, the entire New Testament was translated into Cherokee.

In 1827, type was ordered cast in the characters of the syllabary for a printing press to be established at New Echota, the Cherokee capital. That same year, the council adopted a national constitution, and early in 1828 the Cherokee *Phoenix* began publication. "With a constitution and na-

Civilization had now progressed so far among the Cherokee that in the fall of 1820 they adopted a regular republican form of government modeled after that of the United States. Under this arrangement the nation was divided into eight districts, each of which was to send four representatives to the Cherokee national legislature, which met at Newtown, or New Echota, the capital, at the junction of Conasauga and Coosawatee rivers, a few miles above the present Calhoun, Georgia. The legislature consisted of an upper and a lower house, designated, respectively (in the Cherokee language), the national committee and national council, the members being elected for limited terms by the voters of each district. The principal officer was styled president of the national council; the distinguished John Ross was the first to hold this office. There was also a clerk of the committee and two principal members to express the will of the council or lower house. For each district there were appointed a council house for meetings twice a year, a judge, and a marshal. Companies of "light horse" were organized to assist in the execution of the laws, with a "ranger" for each district to look after stray stock. Each head of a family and each single man under the age of sixty was subject to a poll tax. Laws were passed for the collection of taxes and debts, for repairs on roads, for licenses to white persons engaged in farming or other business in the nation, for the support of schools, for the regulation of the liquor traffic and the conduct of negro slaves, to punish horse stealing and theft, to compel all marriages between white men and Indian women to be according to regular legal or church form, and to discourage polygamy. By special decree the right of blood revenge or capital punishment was taken from the seven clans and vested in the constituted authorities of the nation. It was made treason, punishable with death, for any individual to negotiate the sale of lands to the whites without the consent of the national council. White men were not allowed to vote or to hold office in the nation. The system compared favorably with that of the Federal government or of any state government then existing. (Mooney 1900: 106–7)

Fig. 8.3. Reconstructed print shop at New Echota, Gordon County (courtesy Georgia Department of Natural Resources)

tional press, a well-developed system of industries and home education, and a government administered by educated Christian men, the Cherokee were now justly entitled to be considered a civilized people" (Mooney 1900: 113).

Their progress in adapting to the larger society was not favorably viewed by the state governments, particularly that of Georgia. The year 1828 was to prove disastrous for the Cherokees, for in that year Andrew Jackson was elected president. In the same year, word spread of the discovery of gold at Dahlonega, and the area—despite its location on Cherokee land—became the scene of America's first gold rush. Georgia grew more anxious than ever for its final population of native peoples to leave, and with this in mind the legislature passed several laws designed to make the Cherokees increasingly unhappy and thus more willing to leave. One

Fig. 8.4. John Ridge, a Cherokee (courtesy of Hargrett Rare Book and Manuscript Library/University of Georgia Libraries)

such law declared null and void all Cherokee laws within the boundaries of the state of Georgia and extended Georgia laws to all of the Cherokee nation within the state's boundaries. Furthermore, no Indian was allowed to sue a white man, or to act as a witness where a white man was the defendant. Other laws forbade the Cherokees to hold councils, to assemble for any purpose, or to dig for gold on their own land. President Jackson, a firm states' rights advocate, supported Georgia's efforts to oust the Cherokees.

The tribe appealed to the Supreme Court, which ruled in their favor, but President Jackson refused to abide by the court's decision and by his actions encouraged the government of Georgia to proceed in its efforts to rid the state of the Cherokees. In 1835, the Treaty of New Echota was signed, the long-sought treaty of removal, which stipulated that the Cherokees would voluntarily leave within three years or be forcibly removed. The treaty was signed by a few Cherokees who had no legal authority to do so and who did not represent the will of the people. Nevertheless, Congress ratified the treaty (by a one-vote majority), and it became law.

In 1838, President Van Buren inherited the Cherokee problem. Inclined to be more lenient, Van Buren bowed to threats from Governor George Gilmer of Georgia, and ordered General Winfield Scott to head an army to round up the Cherokees. Beginning in the summer of 1838, the Cherokees were held in stockades erected throughout their territory as the troops sought out more members of the tribe. In the fall, they began the journey west on what has aptly been called the "Trail of Tears." It is estimated that as many as 4,000 died on the forced march, including the wife of Chief John Ross. Hundreds had died in the stockades while awaiting removal. But Georgia was at last free of its native inhabitants and could open up their former territory for white settlement. A county carved out of the former Cherokee nation was named in honor of Gilmer, who had been so adamant in his demands for the federal government to see to it that the Cherokees were escorted out of the state.

The departure of the last of Georgia's native peoples did not mean the end of their influence on the state, its people, and their culture. The history of the Indian tribes of Georgia is an important part of the history of the state. Public school textbooks on Georgia history commonly include sections relating to the Indian tribes. Indian influence is also reflected in the names of some of Georgia's counties (Catoosa, Cherokee, Muscogee, Chattooga, Coweta), towns and cities (Tallapoosa, Chickamauga, Willacoochee, Ball Ground), rivers (Ocmulgee, Ogeechee, Altamaha, Coosa, Tugalo, Chattahoochee), and other geographic features. Many roads and highways follow earlier Indian trails. The growing awareness of the state's Indian heritage is reflected in the establishment of several state parks and historic sites, with the primary goal of protecting aboriginal remains and educating visitors about the significance of the site. These include Etowah Mounds (near Cartersville), Kolomoki Mounds (near Blakely), New Echota (near Calhoun), and Indian Springs (near Jackson). In addition, Ocmulgee National Monument at Macon, part of the national park system, provides an excellent opportunity for visitors to learn about Georgia's prehistoric inhabitants. These are all constant and obvious reminders of the first Georgians. However, the native peoples also contributed to Georgia's cultural heritage in other, less obvious, ways.

"Acculturation," a term used by anthropologists, has to do with the process whereby cultures that come into contact exchange ideas, customs, artifacts, and so on. As the Europeans established themselves in Georgia,

---

The history of this Cherokee removal of 1838, as gleaned by the author from the lips of actors in the tragedy, may well exceed in weight of grief and pathos any other passage in American history. Even the much-sung exile of the Acadians falls far behind it in its sum of death and misery. Under Scott's orders the troops were disposed at various points throughout the Cherokee country, where stockade forts were erected for gathering in and holding the Indians preparatory to removal. From these, squads of troops were sent to search out with rifle and bayonet every small cabin hidden away in the coves or by the sides of mountain streams, to seize and bring in as prisoners all the occupants, however or wherever they might be found. Families at dinner were startled by the sudden gleam of bayonets in the doorway and rose up to be driven with blows and oaths along the weary miles of trail that led to the stockade. Men were seized in their fields or going along the road, women were taken from their wheels and children from their play. In many cases, on turning for one last look as they crossed the ridge, they saw their homes in flames, fired by the lawless rabble that followed on the heels of the soldiers to loot and pillage. So keen were these outlaws on the scent that in some instances they were driving off the cattle and other stock of the Indians almost before the soldiers had fairly started their owners in the other direction. Systematic hunts were made by the same men for Indian graves, to rob them of the silver pendants and other valuables deposited with the dead. A Georgia volunteer, afterward a colonel in the Confederate service, said: "I fought through the civil war and have seen men shot to pieces and slaughtered by thousands, but the Cherokee removal was the cruelest work I ever knew." (Mooney 1900: 130)

---

they learned survival techniques from the original inhabitants. This was particularly the case along the frontier in the upper Piedmont and into the Southern Appalachians. Although the frontier was an uncertain and at times dangerous place, there was an exchange of ideas. The European settlers learned some of the hunting, fishing, and gathering strategies of the Indian tribes and incorporated them into their own way of life. Few people realize that some of these practices persisted into the twentieth century. Especially during the Great Depression of the 1930s, rural people supplemented the food they raised in their fields and gardens with food obtained through hunting, fishing, and gathering. Aboriginal techniques were often used in these pursuits, for they apparently do not have counterparts in the traditional cultures of Europe. The environment was quite different from that of Europe, and Georgia's plants and animals had to be procured by different means. Particularly in the case of edible wild plants, Europeans had to learn from the native tribes, who had used these food sources for millennia.

I found a good example of aboriginal subsistence techniques used by rural white populations several years ago when I was conducting ethnohistoric research in the upper Piedmont of Georgia. Elderly informants recalled that in their youth they hunted birds by shooting them with darts propelled from a blowgun. In autumn, migrating blackbirds would roost in canebrakes along the rivers. Boys would take their blowguns into the canebrakes at night, shooting the birds by torchlight. This was an efficient way of hunting, for there was no noise to frighten the birds. The blackbirds made a tasty addition to the diet.

Native plants gathered in season also supplemented agricultural produce. American chestnuts were a favorite, along with other seasonal products such as blackberries, huckleberries, wild strawberries, and pokeweed (gathered when the shoots first appear in early spring). By following some of these aboriginal subsistence practices, the European settlers and their descendants not only survived but prospered.

The fact remains, however, that Georgia has no native peoples today, except for those few who have moved from other states and who represent a number of tribes, including the Mohawk, Sioux, Pueblo, Eastern Cherokee, Oklahoma Cherokee, and Tuscarora. The governments of Georgia and the United States were thorough in ridding the state of its native inhabitants. The greed, prejudice, and often violent hatred exhibited by the state's leaders and many of its citizens ensured that there would be no

The Cherokees are nearly all prisoners. They have been dragged from their houses and encamped at the forts and military posts, all over the Nation. In Georgia, especially, the most unfeeling and insulting treatment has been experienced by them, in a general way. Multitudes were not allowed time to take any thing with them, but the clothes they had on. Well furnished houses, were left a prey to plunderers, who, like hungry wolves, follow the progress of the captors and, in many cases, accompany them. These wretches rifle the houses and strip the helpless, unoffending owners of all they have on earth. Females, who have been habituated to comforts, and comparative affluence are driven on foot before the bayonets of brutal men. Their feelings are mortified by the blasphemous vociferations of these heartless captors. It is a painful sight. The property of many have been taken, and sold before their eyes, for almost nothing; the sellers and buyers being, in many cases, combined to cheat the poor Indians. Private purchases, or at least the sham of purchases, have, in many instances, been made, at the instant of arrest & consternation: the soldiers standing with their guns and bayonets, impatient to go on with their work, could give but little time to transact business. The poor captive in a state of distressing agitation, his weeping wife almost frantic with terror, surrounded by a group of crying, terrified children without a friend to speak one consoling word, is in a very unfavorable condition to make advantageous disposition of his property, even were suitable and honest purchasers on the spot: but more especially so, when the only purchasers present are … [compared?] … not … [contrasted?], in said villany, to the watchers, who plunder the ship-wrecked voyager, on the sea coast. The truth is, the Cherokees are, deprived of their liberty and stripped of their intire property at one blow. Many, who a few days ago, were in comfortable circumstances, are now, the victims of abject poverty. Many, who have been allowed to return to their homes under passport to enquire after their property, have found their horses, cattle, hogs, ploughs, hoes, harness, tables, chairs, an[d] other ware: all gone. And this is not a description of extreme cases. It is altogether a faint and feeble representation, of the work of barbarity which has been perpetrated on the unoffending, unarmed and unresisting Cherokees. (Rev. Evan Jones, June 16, 1838, quoted in Gardner 1989:212–13; reprinted courtesy of Robert Gardner)

Indian presence. Yet, while the Indian tribes who once lived in Georgia are gone, we must never forget them. Their legacy is part of Georgia's heritage. It is my desire that all Georgians develop a greater appreciation for those who were here first.

Suggestions for Further Reading

Debo, Angie. 1941. *The Road to Disappearance: A History of the Creek Indians.* Norman: University Of Oklahoma Press.

Ehle, John. 1988. *Trail of Tears: The Rise and Fall of the Cherokee Nation.* New York: Anchor Press.

Gardner, Robert G. 1989. *Cherokees and Baptists in Georgia.* Atlanta: Georgia Baptist Historical Society.

Bibliography

Adair, James. [1930] 1974. *Adair's History of the American Indians,* ed. Samuel Cole Williams. New York: Promontory Press.

Alterman, Michael L. 1983. "An Evaluation of the Piedmont Late Archaic along the Upper Savannah River Valley." Paper presented at the meeting of the Society for American Archaeology, Pittsburgh.

Anderson, David G. 1990. "The Paleoindian Colonization of Eastern North America: A View from the Southeastern United States." *Research in Economic Anthropology,* Supplement 5: 163–216.

Anderson, David G., and Glen T. Hanson. 1988. "Early Archaic Settlement in the Southeastern United States: A Case Study from the Savannah River Valley." *American Antiquity* 53, 2: 262–86.

Anderson, David G., and Joseph Schuldenrein. 1985. *Prehistoric Human Ecology along the Upper Savannah River: Excavations at the Rucker's Bottom, Abbeville, and Bullard Site Groups.* Vol. 2. Russell Papers. Atlanta: Archeological Services Branch, National Park Service.

Anderson, David G., and Kenneth E. Sassaman. 1996. *The Paleoindian and Early Archaic Southeast.* Tuscaloosa: University of Alabama Press.

Anderson, David G., R. Jerald Ledbetter, and Lisa O'Steen. 1990. *Paleoindian Period Archaeology of Georgia.* Georgia Archaeological Research Design Papers 6. Athens: University of Georgia Laboratory of Archaeology.

Bartram, William. [1928] 1955. *Travels of William Bartram,* ed. Mark Van Doren. Originally published 1791. New York: Dover.

———. [1853] 1976. "Observations on the Creek and Cherokee Indians." *Transactions of the American Ethnological Society.* Vol. 3, pt. 1. Millwood, N.Y.: Kraus Reprint.

Begley, Sharon, and Andrew Murr. 1999. "The First Americans." *Newsweek,* April 26, 50–57.

Bense, Judith A. 1994. *Archaeology of the Southeastern United States*. San Diego: Academic Press.

Bowne, Eric E. 2000. "The Rise and Fall of the Westo Indians: An Evaluation of the Documentary Evidence." *Early Georgia* 28, 1: 56–78.

Braly, Chad O. 1995. *Historic Indian Period Archaeology of the Georgia Coastal Plain*. Report 34. Athens: University of Georgia Laboratory of Archaeology.

Braun, E. Lucy. 1967. *Deciduous Forests of Eastern North America*. New York: Hafner.

Brockington, Paul. 1971. "A Preliminary Investigation of an Early Knapping Site in Southeastern Georgia." *Notebook* 3: 34–46. Columbia: Institute of Archaeology and Anthropology, University of South Carolina.

Bullen, Ripley P., and H. Bruce Green. 1970. "Stratigraphic Tests at Stalling's Island, Georgia." *Florida Anthropologist* 23, 1: 8–28.

Burleigh, Thomas D. 1958. *Georgia Birds*. Norman: University of Oklahoma Press.

Caldwell, Joseph. 1958. *Trend and Tradition in the Prehistory of the Eastern United States*. American Anthropological Association Memoir 88.

Caldwell, Joseph, and Catherine McCann. 1941. *Irene Mound Site, Chatham County, Georgia*. Athens: University of Georgia Press.

Campbell, L. Janice, and Prentice M. Thomas, Jr. 1981. "Late Archaic Occupations in the Sand Hills Region of Georgia: Application of the Focal-Diffuse Model." Paper presented at the Southeastern Archaeological Conference, Asheville, N.C.

Campbell, L. Janice, and Carol S. Weed, eds. 1984. *The Beaverdam Group: Archaeological Investigations at 9EB92, 9EB207, 9EB208, and 9EB219, Richard Russell B. Multiple Resource Area, Elbert County, Georgia*. Russell Papers. Atlanta: Archeological Services Branch, National Park Service.

Claflin, William H., Jr. 1931. "The Stalling's Island Mound, Columbia County, Georgia." *Papers of the Peabody Museum of American Archaeology and Ethnology, Harvard University* 14, 1: 1–47.

Clausen, C. J., A. D. Cohen, Cesare Emiliani, J. A. Holman, and J. J. Stipp. 1979. "Little Salt Spring, Florida: A Unique Underwater Site." *Science*, February 16, 609–14.

➤ Clayton, Lawrence A., Vernon James Knight, Jr., and Edward C. Moore, eds. 1993. *The De Soto Chronicles: The Expedition of Hernando de Soto to North America in 1539–1543*. Vol. 1. Tuscaloosa: University of Alabama Press.

Cobb, Charles R., and Patrick H. Garrow. 1996. "Woodstock Culture and the Question of Mississippian Emergence." *American Antiquity* 61, 1: 21–37.

Coe, Joffre L. 1964. *The Formative Cultures of the Carolina Piedmont*. Philadelphia: Transactions of the American Philosophical Society, n.s. 54.

➤ Coleman, Kenneth, ed. 1991. *A History of Georgia*. Athens: University of Georgia Press.

Cook, Fred C. 1977. "The Lower Georgia Coast as a Cultural Sub-Region." *Early Georgia* 5, 1–2: 15–36.

———. 1979. "Kelvin: A Late Woodland Phase on the Southern Georgia Coast." *Early Georgia* 7, 2: 65–86.

Crane, Verner W. 1928. *The Southern Frontier, 1670–1732.* Durham, N.C.: Duke University Press.

Crook, Morgan R., Jr. 1984. *Cagle Site Report: Archaic and Early Woodland Period Manifestations in the North Georgia Piedmont.* Occasional Papers in Cultural Resource Management 2. Atlanta: Georgia Department of Transportation, Office of Environmental Analysis.

———. 1986. *Mississippi Period Archaeology of the Georgia Coastal Zone.* Report 23. Athens: University of Georgia Laboratory of Archaeology.

Crusoe, Donald L., and Chester B. DePratter. 1976. "A New Look at the Georgia Coastal Shell Mound Archaic." *Florida Anthropologist* 29, 1: 1–23.

Dahlberg, Michael D. 1975. *Guide to Coastal Fishes of Georgia and Nearby States.* Athens: University of Georgia Press.

Delcourt, Paul A., and Hazel R. Delcourt. 1987. *Long-Term Forest Dynamics of the Temperate Zone.* New York: Springer-Verlag.

———. 1998. "Paleoecological Insights on Conservation of Biodiversity: A Focus on Species, Ecosystems, and Landscapes." *Ecological Applications* 8, 4: 921–34.

Debo, Angie. 1941. *The Road to Disappearance: A History of the Creek Indians.* Norman: University of Oklahoma Press.

DePratter, Chester B. 1975. "The Archaic in Georgia." *Early Georgia* 3, 1: 1–16.

———. 1976. "The Refuge Phase on the Coastal Plain of Georgia." *Early Georgia* 4: 1–13.

———. 1977. "Environmental Changes on the Georgia Coast During the Prehistoric Period." *Early Georgia* 5, 1–2: 1–14.

Ehle, John. 1988. *Trail of Tears: The Rise and Fall of the Cherokee Nation.* New York: Anchor Press.

Fairbanks, Charles H. 1946. "The Macon Earth Lodge." *American Antiquity* 12: 94–108.

———. 1956. *Archeology of the Funeral Mound, Ocmulgee National Monument, Georgia.* Archeological Research Series 3. Washington: National Park Service.

Fenneman, Nevin M. 1938. *Physiography of Eastern United States.* New York: McGraw Hill.

Ferguson, Leland G. 1974. "Prehistoric Mica Mines in the Southern Appalachians." *South Carolina Antiquities* 2: 211–217.

Fish, Paul Robert, and William W. Mitchell. 1976. *Late Archaic Settlement in the Big Slough Watershed.* Report 13. Athens: University of Georgia Laboratory of Archaeology.

Gardner, Robert G. 1989. *Cherokees and Baptists in Georgia.* Atlanta: Georgia Baptist Historical Society.

Garrow, Patrick H. 1975. "The Woodland Period North of the Fall Line." *Early Georgia* 3, 1: 17–26.

———. 2000. "The Woodland Period North of the Fall Line." Paper presented at the Southeastern Archaeological Conference, Macon, Ga.

Gilbert, William H., Jr. 1943. *The Eastern Cherokees*. Bureau of American Ethnology Bulletin 133, Anthropological Papers 23. Washington: Government Printing Office.

Goad, Sharon I. 1979. *Chert Resources in Georgia: Archaeological and Geological Perspectives*. Report 21. Athens: University of Georgia Laboratory of Archaeology.

Golley, Frank B. 1962. *Mammals of Georgia*. Athens: University of Georgia Press.

Goodyear, Albert C. 1999. "Results of the 1999 Allendale Paleoindian Expedition." *Legacy* 4, 1–3: 8–13.

Goodyear, Albert C., James L. Michie, and Barbara A. Purdy. 1980. "The Edgefield Scraper: A Distributional Study of an Early Archaic Stone Tool from the Southeastern U.S." Paper presented at the meeting of the Southeastern Archaeological Conference, New Orleans.

Gresham, Thomas H. 1990. "Historic Patterns of Rock Piling and the Rock Pile Problem." *Early Georgia* 18, 1–2: 1–40.

Hally, David J. 1993. "The 1992 and 1993 Excavations at the King Site (9FL5)." *Early Georgia* 21, 2: 30–44.

———, ed. 1994. *Ocmulgee Archaeology, 1936–1986*. Athens: University of Georgia Press.

Hally, David J., and James B. Langford, Jr. 1988. *Mississippi Period Archaeology of the Georgia Valley and Ridge Province*. Report 25. Athens: University of Georgia Laboratory of Archaeology.

Hally, David J., and James L. Rudolph. 1986. *Mississippi Period Archaeology of the Georgia Piedmont*. Report 24. Athens: University of Georgia Laboratory of Archaeology.

Hann, John H. 1996. *History of the Timucua Indians and Missions*. Gainesville: University Press of Florida.

Harrell, Sara Gordon. 1977. *Tomo-chi-chi*. Minneapolis: Dillon Press.

Hawkins, Benjamin. 1848. *A Sketch of the Creek Country in 1798 and 1799*. Georgia Historical Society Collections, vol. 3, pt. 1. Savannah.

———. 1916. *Letters of Benjamin Hawkins, 1796–1806*. Georgia Historical Society Collections, vol. 9. Savannah.

Heye, George G., F. W. Hodge, and G. H. Pepper. 1918. *The Nacoochee Mound in Georgia*. Contributions from the Heye Museum of the American Indian 2, 1. New York.

Hoffman, Paul E. 1994. "Lucas Vázquez de Ayllón's Discovery and Colony." In *The Forgotten Centuries: Indians and Europeans in the American South, 1521–1704*, ed. Charles Hudson and Carmen Chaves Tesser, 36–49. Athens: University of Georgia Press.

Hudson, Charles. 1997. *Knights of Spain, Warriors of the Sun*. Athens: University of Georgia Press.

Hudson, Charles, and Carmen Chaves Tesser, eds. 1994. *The Forgotten Centuries: Indians and Europeans in the American South, 1521–1704*. Athens: University of Georgia Press.

Huscher, Harold A. 1964. "The Standing Boy Flint Industry: An Early Archaic Manifestation of the Chattahoochee River in Alabama and Georgia." *Southern Indian Studies* 16: 3–20.

Jefferies, Richard W. 1976. *The Tunacunnhee Site: Evidence of Hopewell Interaction in Northwest Georgia*. Anthropological Papers of the University of Georgia, no. 1. Athens: Anthropology Department, University of Georgia.

Jones, Charles C., Jr. 1868. *Historical Sketch of Tomo-chi-chi, Mico of the Yamacraws*. Albany, N.Y.: Joel Munsell.

Kellar, James H., A. R. Kelly, and Edward V. McMichael. 1962. "The Mandeville Site in Southwest Georgia." *American Antiquity* 27, 3: 336–55.

Kelly, A. R. 1938. *A Preliminary Report on Archaeological Explorations at Macon, Georgia*. Bureau of American Ethnology Bulletin 119, Anthropological Papers 1. Washington: Government Printing Office.

———. 1939. "The Macon Trading Post, An Historical Foundling." *American Antiquity* 4, 4: 328–33.

———. 1950. "An Early Flint Industry in Southwest Georgia." In *Short Contributions to the Geology, Geography, and Archaeology of Georgia*. Geological Survey Bulletin 56, 146–153. Atlanta: Department of Mines, Mining, and Geology, State Division of Conservation.

———. 1954. "The Eatonton Effigy Eagle Mounds and Related Stone Structures in Putnam County, Georgia." *Georgia Mineral Newsletter* 7, 2: 82–86.

———. 1973. "Early Villages on the Chattahoochee River, Georgia." *Archaeology* 26, 1: 32–37.

Kelly, A. R., and Lewis H. Larson, Jr. 1956. "Explorations at Etowah Indian Mounds near Cartersville, Georgia, Seasons 1954, 1955, 1956." *Archaeology* 10: 39–48.

King, Adam. 1995. *Steps to the Past: 1994 Archaeological Excavations at Mounds A and B at the Etowah Site (9Br1), Bartow County, Georgia*. Atlanta: Georgia Department of Natural Resources.

LaForge, Laurence, et al. 1925. *Physical Geography of Georgia*. Geological Survey of Georgia, Bulletin 42. Atlanta: Department of Mines, Mining, and Geology.

Larsen, Clark Spencer, and David Hurst Thomas. 1982. *The Anthropology of St. Catherines Island 4: The St. Catherines Period Mortuary Complex*. Anthropological Papers of the American Museum of Natural History, vol. 57, pt. 4. New York.

———. 1986. *The Archaeology of St. Catherines Island 5: The South End Mound Complex*. Anthropological Papers of the American Museum of Natural History, vol. 63, pt. 1. New York.

Larson, Lewis H., Jr. 1959. "A Mississippian Headdress from Etowah, Georgia." *American Antiquity* 25, 1: 109–12.

———. 1971. "Archaeological Implications of Social Stratification at the Etowah Site, Georgia." In *Approaches to the Social Dimensions of Mortuary Practices*, ed. James A. Brown, 58–67. Memoirs of the Society for American Archaeology 25. Washington, D.C.: Society for American Archaeology.

Ledbetter, R. Jerald. 1997. *The Bull Creek Site, 9ME1, Muscogee County, Georgia*. Occasional Papers in Cultural Resource Management 9. Atlanta: Georgia Department of Transportation.

Lepionka, Larry. 1983. "The Early Woodland Ceramic Typology of the Second Refuge Site, Jasper County, South Carolina." *South Carolina Antiquities* 15, 1–2: 17–30.

Lewis, Thomas M. N., and Madeline Kneberg Lewis. 1961. *Eva, An Archaic Site*. University of Tennessee Study in Anthropology. Knoxville: University of Tennessee Press.

Lipps, Lewis, and Clayton E. Ray. 1967. "The Pleistocene Fossiliferous Deposit at Ladds, Bartow County, Georgia." *Bulletin of the Georgia Academy of Science* 25, 3: 113–19.

Little, Keith J. 1985. "A Sixteenth Century European Sword from a Proto-historic Aboriginal Site in Northwest Georgia." *Early Georgia* 13, 1–2: 1–14.

Malone, Henry T. 1956. *Cherokees of the Old South*. Athens: University of Georgia Press.

Mereness, Newton D., ed. 1916. *Travels in the American Colonies*. New York: Macmillan.

Milanich, Jerald T. 1972. "The Deptford Phase: An Adaptation of Hunting-Gathering Bands to the Southeastern Coastal Strand." *Southeastern Archaeological Conference Bulletin* 15, 21–23.

———. 1980. "Coastal Georgia Deptford Culture: Growth of a Concept." In *Excursions in Southeastern Geology: The Archaeology-Geology of the Georgia Coast*, ed. James D. Howard, Chester B. DePratter, and Robert W. Frey, 170–78. Guidebook 20, Georgia Geological Survey. Atlanta: Environmental Protection Division, Department of Natural Resources.

———. 2000. "The Timucua Indians of Northern Florida and Southern Georgia." In *Indians of the Greater Southeast*, ed. Bonnie G. McEwan, 1–25. Gainesville: University Press of Florida.

Mooney, James. 1900. "Myths of the Cherokees." *Bureau of American Ethnology 19th Annual Report, Pt. 1, 1897–98*. Washington: Government Printing Office.

Moorehead, Warren K. [1932] 1979. *Etowah Papers*. Andover, Mass.: Department of Archaeology, Phillips Academy.

O'Connor, Mallory McCane. 1995. *Lost Cities of the Ancient Southeast*. Gainesville: University Press of Florida.

O'Steen, Lisa D., R. Jerald Ledbetter, and Daniel T. Elliott. 1983. "Paleoindian Sites of the Inner Piedmont of Georgia and South Carolina." Paper presented at the Southeastern Archaeological Conference, Columbia, S.C.

Pluckhahn, Thomas J. 1997. *An Archaeological Survey of the Shoulderbone Tract, Hancock County, Georgia.* Occasional Papers in Cultural Resource Management 10. Atlanta: Georgia Department of Transportation.

———. 1998. *Highway 61 Revisited: Archaeological Evaluation of Eight Sites in Bartow County, Georgia.* Athens, Ga.: Southeastern Archaeological Services.

Price, T. Jeffrey. 1994. *An Archaeological Resource Survey of Proposed Widening along State Route 61, Bartow County, Georgia.* Athens, Ga.: Southeastern Archaeological Services.

Russo, Michael. 1996. "Southeastern Mid-Holocene Coastal Settlements." In *Archaeology of the Mid-Holocene South,* ed. Kenneth E. Sassaman and David G. Anderson, 177–99. Gainesville: University Press of Florida.

Sassaman, Kenneth E. 1996. "Technological Innovations in Economic and Social Contexts." In *Archaeology of the Mid-Holocene South,* ed. Kenneth E. Sassaman and David G. Anderson, 57–74. Gainesville: University Press of Florida.

Schnell, Frank T., and Newell O. Wright, Jr. 1993. *Mississippi Period Archaeology of the Georgia Coastal Plain.* Report 26. Athens: University of Georgia Laboratory of Archaeology.

Schnell, Frank T., Vernon J. Knight, Jr., and Gail S. Schnell. 1981. *Cemochechobee: Archaeology of a Mississippian Ceremonial Center on the Chattahoochee River.* Gainesville: University Presses of Florida.

Sears, William H. 1956. *Excavations at Kolomoki: Final Report.* University of Georgia Series in Anthropology, No. 5. Athens: University of Georgia Press.

Shelford, Victor E. 1963. *The Ecology of North America.* Urbana: University of Illinois Press.

Simpkins, Daniel L. 1975. "A Preliminary Report on Test Excavations at the Sapelo Island Shell Ring, 1975." *Early Georgia* 3, 2: 15–37.

Smith, Betty A. 1977. "Southwest Georgia Prehistory: An Overview." *Early Georgia* 5, 1–2: 61–72.

———. 1979. "The Hopewell Connection in Southwest Georgia." In *Hopewell Archaeology: The Chillicothe Conference,* ed. David S. Brose and N'omi Greber, 181–87. Kent, Ohio: Kent State University Press.

Smith, Marvin T. 1987. *Archaeology of Aboriginal Culture Change in the Interior Southeast: Depopulation during the Early Historic Period.* Gainesville: University Presses of Florida.

———. 1992. *Historic Period Indian Archaeology of Northern Georgia.* Report 30. Athens: University of Georgia Laboratory of Archaeology.

———. 1994. *Archaeological Investigations at the Dyar Site, 9GE5.* Report 32. Athens: University of Georgia Laboratory of Archaeology.

Smith, Philip E. 1962. *Aboriginal Stone Constructions in the Southern Piedmont.* Report 4, pt. 2. Athens: University of Georgia Laboratory of Archaeology.

Snow, Francis H. 1975. "Swift Creek Designs and Distribution: A South Georgia Study." *Early Georgia* 3, 2: 38–59.

————. 1977. "A Survey of the Ocmulgee Big Bend Region." *Early Georgia* 5, 1–2: 36–60.

Speck, Frank G. 1909. *Ethnology of the Yuchi Indians.* Anthropological Publications of the University Museum, vol. 1, no. 1. Philadelphia: University of Pennsylvania.

Spencer, Robert F., Jesse D. Jennings, et al. 1977. *The Native Americans.* 2d. ed. New York: Harper and Row.

Steinen, Karl. 1977. "Weeden Island in Southwest Georgia." *Early Georgia* 5, 1–2: 73–87.

Stephenson, Keith, Adam King, and Frankie Snow. 1996. "Middle Mississippian Occupation in the Ocmulgee Big Bend Region." *Early Georgia* 24, 2: 1–41.

Stephenson, Keith, John E. Worth, and Frankie Snow. 1990. "A Savannah Period Mound in the Upper-Interior Coastal Plain of Georgia." *Early Georgia* 18, 1–2: 4–64.

Sturtevant, William C. 1996. "The Misconnection of Guale and Yamassee with Muskogean." *International Journal of American Linguistics* 60: 139–48.

Swanton, John R. 1928. "Social Organization and Social Usages of the Indians of the Creek Confederacy." *Bureau of American Ethnology, 42d Annual Report.* Washington: Government Printing Office.

————. 1946. *Indians of the Southeastern United States.* Bureau of American Ethnology Bulletin 137. Washington: Government Printing Office.

————. [1922] 1998. *Early History of the Creek Indians and Their Neighbors.* Gainesville: University Press of Florida.

Thomas, David Hurst. 1993. *Historic Indian Period Archaeology of the Georgia Coastal Zone.* Report 31. Athens: University of Georgia Laboratory of Archaeology.

Thomas, David Hurst, and Clark Spencer Larsen. 1979. *The Anthropology of St. Catherines Island 2: The Refuge-Deptford Mortuary Complex.* Anthropological Papers of the American Museum of Natural History, vol. 56, pt. 1. New York.

Thomas, David Hurst, and Lorann S. A. Pendleton. 1987. *The Archaeology of Mission Santa Catalina de Guale.* Vol. 1, *Search and Discovery.* Anthropological Papers of the American Museum of Natural History, vol. 63, pt. 2. New York.

Thomas, David Hurst, Grant D. Jones, Roger S. Durham, and Clark Spencer Larsen. 1978. *The Anthropology of St. Catherines Island 1: Natural and Cultural History.* Anthropological Papers of the American Museum of Natural History, vol. 55, pt. 2. New York.

Thornbury, William D. 1965. *Regional Geomorphology of the United States.* New York: Wiley.

Tippitt, V. Ann, and William H. Marquardt. 1984. *The Gregg Shoals and Clyde Gulley Sites: Archeological and Geological Investigations at Two Piedmont*

Sites on the Savannah River. Russell Papers. Atlanta: Archeological Services Branch, National Park Service.

Tuck, James A. 1974. "Early Archaic Horizons in Eastern North America." *Archaeology of Eastern North America* 2, 1: 73–80.

Voorhies, M. R. 1971. "The Watkins Quarry: A New Late Pleistocene Mammal Locality in Glynn County, Georgia." *Bulletin of the Georgia Academy of Science* 29, 2.

———. 1974. "Pleistocene Vertebrates with Boreal Affinities in the Georgia Piedmont." *Quaternary Research* 4: 85–93.

Walthall, John A. 1998. "Rockshelters and Hunter-Gatherer Adaptation to the Pleistocene/Holocene Transition." *American Antiquity* 63, 2: 223–38.

Waring, Antonio J., Jr. 1968. *The Waring Papers: The Southern Cult and Other Archaeological Essays,* ed. Stephen Williams. Athens: University of Georgia Press.

Warner, Richard A. 1974. "The Griffin Site: A Stratified Archaic Site from Northwest Georgia." Paper presented at the meeting of the Georgia Academy of Science.

Wauchope, Robert. 1966. *Archaeological Survey of Northern Georgia.* Memoirs of the Society for American Archaeology 21. Salt Lake City: Society for American Archaeology.

Wharton, Charles H. 1978. *The Natural Environments of Georgia.* Atlanta: Georgia Department of Natural Resources.

White, Max E. 1979. "Scotch-Irish Subsistence Practices in the Southern Appalachians." *Irish-American Review* 1, 1: 50–63.

———. 1988. *Georgia's Indian Heritage: The Prehistoric Peoples and Historic Tribes of Georgia.* Roswell, Ga.: Wolfe.

Whitley, David S., and Ronald I. Doren. 1993. "New Perspectives on the Clovis vs. Pre-Clovis Controversy." *American Antiquity* 58, 4: 626–47.

Williams, Mark. 1994. "Archaeological Site Distributions in Georgia: 1994." *Early Georgia* 22, 1: 35–76.

———. 2000. "Archaeological Site Distributions in Georgia: 2000." *Early Georgia* 28, 1: 1–55.

Williams, Mark, and Gary Shapiro. 1990. *Archaeological Excavations at Little River (9MG46), 1984 and 1987.* LAMAR Institute Publications 2. Watkinsville, Ga.

Williams, Mark, and Victor Thompson. 1999. "A Guide to Georgia Indian Pottery Types." *Early Georgia* 27, 1.

Wood, W. Dean, and Dan T. Elliott. 1983. "A Functional Interpretation of Two Late Archaic Sites on the Upper Savannah River." Paper presented at the meeting of the Society for American Archaeology, Pittsburgh.

Worth, John E. 1988. "Mississippian Occupation on the Middle Flint River." Master's thesis, University of Georgia.

———. 1993. *The Struggle for the Georgia Coast: An Eighteenth-Century Spanish Retrospect on Guale and Mocama.* Anthropological Papers of the American Museum of Natural History, no. 75. New York.

———. 1998. *The Timucuan Chiefdoms of Spanish Florida.* Vol. 1, *Assimilation.* Vol. 2, *Resistance and Destruction.* Gainesville: University Press of Florida.

Wright, J. Leitch, Jr. 1986. *Creeks and Seminoles.* Lincoln: University of Nebraska Press.

Wynne, Jack T. 1990. *Mississippi Period Archaeology of the Georgia Blue Ridge Mountains.* Report 27. Athens: University of Georgia Laboratory of Archaeology.

Zurel, Richard, T. Gresham, and David Hally. 1975. *An Archaeological Survey of Channel, Dike, and Streambank Protection Structures, Big Mortar-Snuffbox Swamp Watershed, Long and McIntosh Counties, Georgia.* Research Manuscript 116. Athens: University of Georgia Laboratory of Archaeology.

Index

Max E. White is an associate professor of anthropology at Piedmont College, Demorest, Georgia. He is the author of *Georgia's Indian Heritage*. During the academic year 2001–2002, he was selected as the Governor's Teaching Fellow from Piedmont College.